KID BIZ
YEAR ROUND MONEY-MAKING PROJECTS
FOR YOUNG ENTREPRENEURS

By Bonnie and Noel Drew

EAKIN PRESS ★ **Austin, Texas**

The First Edition of this book
was titled *Fast Cash For Kids*.

Copyright © 1987, 1990
By Bonnie and Noel Drew

Published in the United States of America
By Eakin Press
An Imprint of Eakin Publications, Inc.
P.O. Drawer 90159   ★   Austin, TX 78709-0159

ISBN 0-89015-749-9

Library of Congress Cataloging-in-Publication Data

Drew, Bonnie.
  Kid biz : year round money-making projects for young entrepreneurs / by
Bonnie and Noel Drew.
      p.   cm.
  Previously published as: Fast cash for kids. 1st ed. Seabrook, Tex. : Home-
land Publications, 1987.
  Includes bibliographical references.
  Summary: Explains a variety of projects for children interested in earn-
ing their own money and learning how to manage a business efficiently and
profitably.
  ISBN 0-89015-749-9 : $9.95 (U.S.) ($11.95 Can.)
  1. Money-making projects for children — Juvenile literature. 2. Entre-
preneurship — Juvenile literature. [1. Moneymaking projects. 2. Business enterprises.] I. Drew, Noel. II. Drew, Bonnie. Fast cash for kids.
III. Title.
HF5392.D74   1990
650.1'2--dc20   90-36631
                                                                        CIP
                                                                         AC

To our sons, Jon and Robby,
and all the kids who inspired this book.

A Note Before We Begin

The purpose of this book is to give ideas for spare time money-making projects, to instruct in basic principles of money management and business start-up, and to motivate and inspire young people to top performance.

The authors do not attempt to advise anyone on legal matters or make any guarantees that all ideas contained herein will be workable in every situation. The degree of success on any money-making venture depends solely on each individual. Those who undertake any business activity should be aware of their responsibilities to contact appropriate authorities for information on regulations, taxes, permits, or licenses.

It is also the responsibility of the individual to follow proper health and safety precautions when using the projects suggested in this book. Parents should advise their kids about what projects are safe for them, which areas are okay to work in, and what safety precautions should be taken when dealing with strangers (see "Door-to-Door Safety" tips, page 136).

CONTENTS

TO PARENTS

Sooner or later, every parent hears this question from kids: "How can I earn some money?" This book is your answer. *Kid Biz* contains 101 money-making projects for kids under sixteen who are too young to get a job — or for kids over sixteen who would like the experience of starting their own business.

Having your own money is part of growing up. Parents see it as a necessary step in preparing their children to be independent. Kids say it's all about learning to be your own boss. Both agree money skills are important.

As parents, we want our kids to develop to their fullest potential. It is significant that a very high percentage of today's influential business leaders were involved in their own money-making ventures as children. The skills your young person learns doing the projects in this book will be used throughout adulthood.

But this is more than a book about money. It's a book about recognizing opportunity, setting goals, making plans, and knowing the satisfaction of a job well done. It teaches kids to think for themselves and gives them hundreds of practical suggestions for handling their own finances.

Our goal is to make earning money a fun and exciting adventure. All we ask from parents is that you give kids a chance to learn by doing. Listen to their plans, make a few suggestions when necessary, and let them try out their ideas. Praise every effort, for there is no failure — only learning and growing.

TO KIDS

Money. We all need it. We all want it. And we all enjoy it when we have it!

What would you do if you got $100 in the mail today? You probably already have a list of things you are wishing for: things you need, things you want, hobbies to try, places to go.

Since you probably don't get $100 in the mail every day, where *do* you get money? Allowances and gifts are how most kids begin to get money. These are good ways, but the size of most allowances is limited. And you never know when gifts will come. You may find some money or win money in a contest. But you need better ways to receive money as you get older.

Money helps you be more in control of your life, and that's what we all want! We love being our own boss! If you want to be more in charge of your life, you want to earn your own money. But *how?*

This book is the answer. Employ yourself! You may be too young to get a job, but you're never too young to start your own business. With these 101 ideas for businesses, you can start right away. And hundreds of how-to suggestions will help you be a success.

What do you do to start a business? Well, you're working on the first thing right now: read this book all the way through. After you've got a picture of the whole plan, follow the steps in Chapters 1, 2, and 3 to start your exciting adventure of being an inventor of business — a young entrepreneur.

CHAPTER 1

HOW TO INVENT A BUSINESS

Does this sound like you? You want to earn some money, but you're too young to get a job. *Or* you are old enough to get a job, but it's hard to work and go to school. Will you always be broke?

Starting your own business may be the answer. Employ yourself! You can work as much or as little as you want, have the spending money you need, and enjoy the fun of being your own boss. You can call yourself a young entrepreneur.

What is an entrepreneur?

The dictionary gives this definition:

Entrepreneur (ahn' tra pra nur): A person who organizes and manages a business undertaking, assuming the risk for the sake of profit.

What does that mean? In short, an entrepreneur is a businessperson who does these things:

(1) Sees an opportunity
(2) Makes a plan
(3) Starts the business
(4) Manages the business
(5) Receives the profit

In other words, an entrepreneur is an *inventor* of a business. That business can be anything from a large corporation like Ford Motor Company to the kids' lemonade stand on your corner.

The 1990s are being called "The Decade of the Entrepreneur." More young people than ever before will launch a business. If you're ready to get started on your future, these are the steps:

    (1) Discover money-making opportunities.
    (2) Choose the right opportunity for you.
    (3) Create a business plan.

<h2 style="text-align:center">STEP 1.</h2>

How to Find Money-Making Opportunity Everywhere You Go

If we called you and said there was a $10 bill in your front yard, would you go out and look for it? Of course you would!

What if we said there is something in our front yard worth $20, and you could have it if you could find it? What would you do? You'd look for it! Well, there *is* something worth $5, $10, or $20 just outside your front door. Did you notice it today? It's *opportunity!*

Opportunity is a time or occasion that is right for doing something — a good chance. Just outside your front door are opportunities worth cash — lots of it! The secret to finding these opportunities is very simple: look for it.

Here is another very important statement to remember: **You will find what you look for.**

Suppose you are saying to yourself, "There's no way to make money in my neighborhood and I'm bored." Then you walk out your front door and go down the street. Do you see any ways to make money? No! All you see is the same old houses, the same old cars, the same old kids playing in the yard.

Now, let's change the picture. Suppose you are thinking, "There *are* ways to make money in my neighborhood and I'm going to find them!"

What do you see when you walk out the front door this time? Yards to mow, cars to wash, kids to babysit. You see opportunity because you are *looking* for it.

Looking for opportunity never gets boring, because the opportunities are always changing. Those you see in the spring won't be there in the fall. Jobs you see this week may not be available next week. But there will always be *new* money-making opportunities to replace those that are used up.

Capture Good Ideas!

Since opportunities change so often, it is a very good idea to write them down. Then you will be able to remember what you saw and where to go.

Use the form on the next page to help begin your list of money-making opportunities. Your list will keep you excited about your good ideas. And your list is evidence that you are starting to see opportunity like a true entrepreneur.

MONEY-MAKING OPPORTUNITIES

OPPORTUNITY	WHERE	POSSIBLE EARNINGS

Seeing opportunity is the first step toward earning your own money as an entrepreneur. Now you are ready to make some decisions about what you will *do* with those opportunities.

How to Choose the Right Opportunity

Choosing a money-making project is like choosing a hobby. It's fun and exciting — the start of an adventure! It promises a chance to use your talents and to discover more about yourself.

This book is like a catalog of money-making ideas. The ideas are arranged by seasons, beginning with spring, then summer, fall, and winter. All together, there are 101 suggested businesses. Use the projects in three ways:

1. Use projects exactly as written.
2. Change details to work better for you.
3. Combine several projects to make a bigger business.

You can see by now that you have many, many more opportunities than you ever thought possible. You have all the ones on the list you made with the money-making opportunities form. And you have the 101 opportunities in this book.

But you will never earn a penny if you stop here! It takes work to turn good ideas into fast cash.

Your job now is to look closely at all the opportunities, choose one, and start making plans.

ABOUT ME:

What Kind of Business Would I Enjoy?

WHAT I LIKE:
   List your hobbies, activities, special interests
   (gymnastics, skateboarding, music, sports, etc.)

   1.

   2.

   3.

   4.

   5.

WHAT I DO WELL:
   List your skills, talents, special abilities
   (computer, art, cooking, fixing things, etc.)

   1.

   2.

   3.

   4.

   5.

MY WORK EXPERIENCE:
   List jobs you have done before
   (cleaning house, yard work, selling candy, etc.)

   1.

   2.

   3.

   4.

   5.

   6.

I LIKE TO SELL THINGS _____ (yes or no)
I LIKE TO HELP OR PROVIDE SERVICE _____
I LIKE TO WORK WITH PEOPLE _____ ALONE _____

The most important thing to consider when you choose a business idea is: **What would I enjoy?** If you like what you are doing, you will stick with it and make it a success. And when you think about it, with all the opportunities on your list, why spend time doing something you hate?

Take time to answer the questions about yourself on the previous page. (If this is not your book, answer the questions on another sheet of paper, please.)

The about-me worksheet helps you make lists of things you like to do, things you do well, and things you know how to do. These lists are clues to finding the *best* money-making ideas for you.

FOLLOW THESE STEPS TO FIND THE BEST MONEY-MAKING IDEAS FOR YOU:

1. Compare your about-me lists to the money-making opportunities list you started earlier. Do you find any that match? Write the ones that match on a separate sheet of paper. Call these your best ideas list.

2. Compare your about-me lists to the chapter of *Kid Biz* ideas for this time of year. Do you find any that match? List the ones that match on the best ideas list.

If you have carefully considered your opportunities, you now have a very exciting list in your hands — your personal best ideas list! These five to ten ideas are businesses at which you would most likely have success starting and operating.

ABOUT- ME LISTS	KID BIZ IDEAS

ABOUT-ME LISTS

COMPARED TO

KID BIZ IDEAS

RESULT: BEST IDEAS FOR YOU

But we're not through yet. We want to know which is *the one best idea* for you — the right opportunity to choose for now. So get your pen ready. We're going to look at the best ideas list a little closer.

STUDY EACH OPPORTUNITY ON YOUR BEST IDEAS LIST. Ask yourself the questions below, and cross off ideas until you have only one or two left.

1. Is this business idea right for my age?
2. Does this business idea fit with my skills?
3. Is it the right time of year?
4. Do I have enough money to get started? Could I get the money?
5. Do I have enough time for this business?
6. Do I have the equipment I would need? Could I get the equipment?
7. Will this business idea make enough money for the effort it will take?
8. Can I be excited about this idea?

As you get down to only two or three ideas on your best ideas list, the decisions get harder. All of the ideas may be very good and sound like lots of fun to try. But since you need to decide on *one* idea for now, here are some tie-breakers.

TIE-BREAKERS:
1. Which project would I enjoy **the most?**
2. Which would be **the fastest** to get started?
3. Which has the possibility of making **the best** profit for my efforts?

This is great! You have found *the one best* money-making idea for you at this time. And now that you understand this easy system of choosing the right opportunity, you can use it again and again as new opportunities arise throughout the year.

STEP 3.

How to Make a Plan

Putting your chosen "one best money-making opportunity" into action is now your goal. All successful entrepreneurs have goals.

Here's an important question: *Would you go out to practice shooting a bow and arrow without a target?* No! You need something to "aim for." And it's the same with earning money.

You are well on your way to success because you have decided on one money-making project. You have a target. Now you need a plan of action steps to hit the target. Some entrepreneurs spend months making business plans. But we are going to use the short worksheet on the next page to get you going.

11

MY BUSINESS PLAN

NAME OF MY BUSINESS: _____

WHAT MY BUSINESS IS: _____

_____

WHEN I PLAN TO WORK: _____

WHO MY CUSTOMERS WILL BE: _____

_____

HOW I PLAN TO GET CUSTOMERS: _____

_____

_____

PRICES I WILL CHARGE: _____

_____

WHAT TO DO TO GET READY:

     1.

     2.

     3.

     4.

     5.

THINGS I WILL NEED: COST:

     1.

     2.

     3.

     4.

     5.

Note: You will want to use the forms in this book over and over. So please don't write in the book. Instead, write your answers on blank paper, or photocopy the pages you need.

The business plan worksheet is the third step toward becoming an entrepreneur. As you fill in the blanks, you are creating a basic step-by-step plan to get your business started.

Another key to success: Talk to your parents about your plans. You may need permission to use tools, the garage, or other things around the house. Plus, your parents can help you think of ways to make your business more successful.

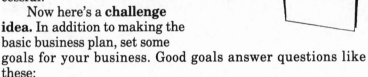

Now here's a **challenge idea.** In addition to making the basic business plan, set some goals for your business. Good goals answer questions like these:

1. How many customers do I want to have?
2. How much money do I want to earn each week, or by a certain date?
3. How much money will I save?

When you set a goal, make it something you can measure. For example: (1) I want to have three regular lawn-mowing jobs each week; (2) I want to earn $45 a week; (3) I want to save half of everything I earn to buy a new skateboard that costs $100.

Make a list of your goals. Get pictures of the skateboard you want. Then ask yourself, "What do I need to do in order to reach these goals?"

GOAL WORKSHEET

LIST THREE GOALS FOR YOUR BUSINESS (things you would like to happen within the next three months):

    1.

    2.

    3.

LIST TWO THINGS YOU NEED TO DO TO MAKE GOAL #1 COME TRUE:

    1.

    2.

LIST TWO THINGS YOU NEED TO DO TO MAKE GOAL #2 COME TRUE:

    1.

    2.

LIST TWO THINGS YOU NEED TO DO TO MAKE GOAL #3 COME TRUE:

    1.

    2.

Setting goals like this makes it easy to get into action making your dreams come true. You may want to use this system to set goals for other interests in your life, or for long-term goals like college or your first car.

In this chapter you learned that anyone who creates a business is an entrepreneur. Then you went through the steps to choose and plan your business. Now it's up to **YOU**. Will you do what it takes to make your dreams come true?

CHAPTER 2

HOW TO GET CUSTOMERS

You've got a hot, money-making idea, you've made a plan, and you've set some goals. You're ready to get started! All you need now is *customers*.

A customer is a person who buys. What does he buy? Your service or product! When will he buy it? When *you* tell him about it.

Telling people about your service or product and getting them to buy it is an important step toward your goal. When you tell — you will sell.

Some businesspeople call the process of telling and selling "marketing." Marketing is everything you do to get customers. It's all the ways you get the message to people about your business.

Big businesses often have whole departments of people whose only job is marketing. But most entrepreneurs start out small like you. They have no employees and they do everything themselves. They **invent** the business and they **market** the business. Once they get customers, they do all the **work**. Then they get all the **pay!**

Entrepreneurs have to know how to do every job in their business. They may work hard, but they like being in control and making the decisions. When the business is a success, they take all the credit!

By now, you are anxious to get busy putting your business ideas into action. We are going to show you how to get people to buy. There are two parts:

1. How to be an expert salesperson.
2. How to advertise your business.

1. How to be an Expert Salesperson

When it comes to selling, no one is as good at it as kids! Kids are the best salespeople in the world!

Did you know that you use salesmanship all the time — every day of your life? You use it on your parents, teachers, brothers and sisters, neighbors, and all of your friends. And no one had to tell you *how* to do it.

You get these folks to do all kinds of things . . . like buying pizza for supper, letting you stay out longer, keeping the puppy that "followed" you home, watching TV shows you like, letting you borrow their stereo, and even giving you their favorite tape for a dumb game no one wants anymore!

Don't tell us you don't know how to sell anything. We *know* you do. But maybe you are like most kids. You never really thought about it that much.

Let's talk about what you do to get people to buy. Suppose you want your mom to buy chocolate-chocolate chip ice cream for dessert tonight. She's watching her weight, and her thoughts are on diet gelatin. How do you convince her to buy the ice cream instead?

These are the steps you use: (We know this is how you do it, because we have two sons who are expert salesmen, and we learned it from them!)

1. **You picture what you want her to buy.**

You think of how good that chocolate ice cream with the little chocolate chips tastes. You picture Mom driving to the store, going straight down the aisle to the ice cream, and choosing chocolate-chocolate chip ice cream for supper tonight.

2. **You expect to talk her into buying it.**

You've convinced her to do many things you've wanted before. You know she likes to do nice things for you. And you believe she will do it — even if she first says no.

3. **You are nice and friendly when you talk to her.**

You tell her exactly what you want and give her that sweet, innocent look that says, "Make me happy, Mom. I'll do anything you say."

4. **You tell her all the reasons she should buy it.**

"Mom, you never buy my kind of ice cream" . . . "Mom, we haven't had anything but diet gelatin for two weeks" . . . "Mom, I'm starving for chocolate-chocolate chip ice cream!"

5. You ask her to buy it now.

"Mom, there's nothing in this house to eat, and I can't survive another minute without some chocolate-chocolate chip ice cream!"

6. If she says no, you go ask your dad!

You realize you've asked the wrong person. Now, your dad is not on a diet and he's tired of that runny green stuff too. He *needs* chocolate-chocolate chip ice cream! So . . . you repeat all of the above steps with your dad, grandma, or other grown-up. And you can *bet* you get chocolate-chocolate chip ice cream for supper tonight!

Look back over the six steps you used to convince Mom to buy chocolate-chocolate chip ice cream. These are the very same steps you will use to sell your product or service to a customer.

Suppose you have started a pet sitting business. Your neighbors are going on vacation and will need someone to take care of their dog Rex.

Let's go through the steps again as if you are talking to a customer about a job.

Step 1: Picture what you want.

Be definite about your goal. You want to earn money doing something you enjoy — pet sitting. You want your neighbors to hire you for the job.

Step 2: Expect them to say yes.

Most adults like to help kids. Don't be shy about speaking up and saying what you want. Be a go-getter who expects to be successful.

Step 3: Be friendly and courteous.

Use your best manners, put a smile on your face, and look well-groomed. The way you look and speak tells people you will do a good job.

Step 4: Tell how your product or service will help.

"You won't have to worry about Rex while you're gone. I know just how to take care of him. We're good friends!" Explain the good points about what you're selling and it will sell itself.

Step 5: Ask the customer to buy now.

There are many ways to get people to decide to buy. Most kids find that just *asking* in simple words is best. The trick is to get them to buy *now*. Here are some interesting ways you may have heard other salespeople get folks to buy now:

"Good for a limited time only!"
"Everyone else is doing it!"
"It's a bargain — they're selling fast!"
"Be the first one to try it!"
"Don't go another day without it!"
"Only three more shopping days 'til . . ."

If you want people to buy now, avoid asking with a question that can be answered yes or no: "May I take care of Rex?" Instead, ask a question that takes for granted they are saying yes: "Do you want me to start feeding Rex today or tomorrow?"

Step 6: If the customer says no, don't give up.

No doesn't always mean no. Sometimes it means they need more information. Think ahead about why people say no and what you can do to change their minds. Here are some ideas:

WHY PEOPLE SAY NO:

1. They don't understand.
2. They aren't sure they will like your product.
3. They are afraid to spend the money.
4. They don't have time right now.
5. They don't have the money right now.
6. They have already hired someone else.
7. They don't need it.

WHAT YOU CAN DO:

1. Give more information.
2. Show how it works and let them try it.
3. Tell them about your other happy customers.
4. Ask if you can come back another time.
5. Offer to take something in trade.
6. Ask them to call if they need you later.
7. Ask if they know someone who needs it.

One way to get more folks to say yes is this: *Ask the ones* **first** *who are* **most** *likely to need or want what you have to offer.* These are called your **target customers.**

Before you start a money-making project, spend some time thinking about your target customers:

Who needs what I am selling?
Who would like what I am selling?
Where will I find these people?

Use the worksheet on the next page to identify your target customers and start a card file. Then use the outline on the following page to plan your sales talk.

MY SALES PLANS

I. WHO ARE MY TARGET CUSTOMERS?

IDENTIFY PEOPLE WHO NEED YOUR PRODUCT
(Dog owners? Mothers of small children? Senior adults? Over-
weight people? Kids?):

_____

_____

IDENTIFY WHERE YOU MIGHT FIND THESE PEOPLE
(PTA meetings? Pet shops? Tennis courts? School? Shopping
centers? Community centers?):

_____

_____

LIST NAMES OF TARGET CUSTOMERS YOU KNOW
(Friends, relatives, former customers, etc.):

1.	8.
2.	9.
3.	10.
4.	11.
5.	12.
6.	13.
7.	14.

START A CARD FILE ON TARGET CUSTOMERS. At the top
of each card write the customer's name, address, and phone
number. Then make notes about pets, children, hobbies, what
they last bought from you, favorite colors, and special requests.
Each time you contact the customer write down the date, result, and when you should contact them again.

MY SALES PLANS

II. WHAT WILL I SAY TO CUSTOMERS?

1. WRITE OUT A SIMPLE INTRODUCTION. (Tell about yourself, your business, and what you are selling.)

2. TELL ABOUT YOUR PRODUCT. (Explain what it is, how it works, special features, colors, etc.)

3. LIST THE BENEFITS OF THE PRODUCT. (People want to buy things that improve their home, make work easier, save time, make them beautiful, etc.)

4. WRITE OUT HOW YOU WILL ASK PEOPLE TO BUY NOW. (Example: Would you prefer to order one or take advantage of our special price on three?)

5. PLAN WHAT TO DO IF THEY SAY NO. (Always leave on a positive note. They might say yes next time!)

6. PLAN WHAT TO DO IF THEY SAY YES. (Always say thanks and do what you promised.)

Even the most expert salespeople are told no. After all, it's not likely that *everyone* will say yes, is it? So there is no reason to feel defeated. You have a good product and a good plan. Your job is to go on telling and selling until you find the ones who are waiting to say *yes*.

There's no doubt about it. Some people are going to say yes. What will you do then?

Step 7: When they say yes, do what you promised!

- Deliver a good product. Do a good job. Be quick, dependable, and helpful.
- Show interest in the needs of the customer. Do something extra, if possible.
- Above all, remember to say thank you.
- Always ask about coming back again. Some people will become your regular customers and buy from you again and again. Do something special for them.

Talking to customers person-to-person is the best way to get a job or sell your product. However, there are other ways to get jobs.

1. *Work for your parents.* Most kids start out this way. Parents are the main employers of kids.
2. *Get someone to ask FOR you.* Your parents or other family members may help by telling people about your business. It helps to be recommended by adults.
3. *Get a partner.* Some kids find it easier to speak to customers with a friend along. Working with friends can be more fun too.
4. *Get customers to call YOU.* Announce your business to the community with flyers, cards, and signs. Your customers will come to you.

2. How to Advertise Your Business

As you read through the 101 money-making projects in this book, you will notice we talk a lot about how to get customers. That's because *you have to have customers to have a business!* Advertising is a very important part of increasing your business.

Like most entrepreneurs, you are starting out on a very low budget. You may even be starting out with a "zero" budget! Don't worry. We are going to show you how to get your advertising almost *free*.

The "Basic Three" Tools of Advertising For the Young Entrepreneur

1. Signs: Use yard signs, banners, and posters where you have big spaces to advertise. They work best for advertising garage sales, yard work, washing cars, firewood for sale, and pool cleaning.

2. Flyers: An artfully designed flyer is probably your number-one best way of advertising. These one sheet advertisements can be given to customers, left on front doors, and placed on bulletin boards all over your community.

3. Cards: Business cards are mini-advertisements you can take anywhere you go. You can make your own or spend about $20 to have 1,000 printed at a copy shop. Cards will make you look and feel more professional. They can be tacked up almost anywhere or handed directly to business contacts.

Low-cost Advertising Tips

1. Before you spend any money on supplies to make signs or flyers, look around your house for things you can use: leftover school supplies, cardboard boxes, poster paints, ink markers, colored paper, and index cards.

2. Save money on printing by using your computer to design and print flyers, banners, and business cards.

3. If you plan to pay for photocopying, compare prices. Cost per page can vary from $0.03 each to $0.15 each.

4. Get good ideas for flyers by studying ads in newspapers and magazines. Save flyers from other businesses in an "idea" folder.

Good Advertising Doesn't Have to be Expensive

Sometimes being low on money can inspire you to be more creative with what you have. Go ahead and make handmade flyers! People will remember you longer for your imagination than a high-cost print job. They can see you are a determined and hard-working young entrepreneur.

The best advertising is absolutely free. Here are two examples:

1. *Word-of-Mouth:* Your happy customers telling others about your business.
2. *Networking:* Friends helping friends. Who do you know that might be helpful in getting the word out that you have started a business?

How to Have Fun With Advertising

· **Wear your ad:** Use fabric paints to create a T-shirt advertising your business. Consider putting your business name on other things such as caps, visors, wind-breakers, and sweat shirts.

· **Use attention-getters:** Put balloons on the yard sign for your toy sale. Wear a pumpkin costume when you sell tickets to your Halloween party. Pass out funny buttons advertising your business. Forget the usual sales talk, and sing a rap song to sell your home-baked cookies.

· **Give freebies:** Pass out coupons for one hour of free babysitting or a half-price car wash. Do free demonstrations of window washing. Hook 'em with free samples of your homemade candy.

· **Find unlikely places:** Put a sign on your bike or in your car window. Ask a teacher to put your flyers in the teacher's lounge.

· **Go public:** Tell your story in the school newspaper or get written up in your community newsletter. If you're doing something unusual, send a letter and pictures to the local newspapers.

What about paid advertising? Don't waste your money by advertising too far away from home unless you have transportation or want to draw customers for a large event like a garage sale.

This chapter is full of excellent ideas to market your business. Spend some time making a list of all the ways you plan to get customers. The best plan is a combination of many ideas.

CHAPTER 3

HOW TO HANDLE YOUR MONEY BUSINESS

What makes a business a business? Lots of kids mow yards, wash cars, sell lemonade, babysit, and walk dogs to earn money. When does it become a business? *When you manage it like one!*

Managing your business means having a system to handle your money, your work, and your decisions. Here are some signs of a well-organized business:

1. A business name
2. A price list
3. A record-keeping system
4. A budget
5. A schedule

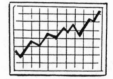

As an entrepreneur, you are in charge of all the decisions about your business. If you want money in the bank, you must run your business like a business. This chapter will tell you how.

1. A Business Name

One of the best ways to let people know you are serious about your money-making plans is to give your business a name. To get some good ideas, look through the yellow pages of your phone book. A good business name tells what you do and makes people remember you.

Things a business name can tell:

1. *What you do:* Maid-for-a-Day
2. *Who owns the business:* Frankie's Crafts
3. *The location:* Main Street Car Wash
4. *Quality of service:* A-OK Cookie Company
5. *Your trademark:* Rainbows Unlimited

After you have chosen a business name, let people know about it. Use it on cards and flyers, paint it on your T-shirt, and say it when you talk to customers. Spread it around!

Next, find a place at home to be your office. It doesn't have to be a large space. A corner of your bedroom or the desk where you do your homework will be fine. Always keep your business papers and supplies in the same place.

Basic supplies for your home office:

1. Note paper, pens, pencils
2. 3 x 5 cards and file box
3. Art or school supplies to make signs and flyers
4. Business cards, printed or handmade
5. Receipt book
6. Notebook to keep records
7. Calculator
8. Envelopes
9. This book
10. Photocopies of forms from this book

You can order return address labels from magazine or newspaper ads for about $3 per 500. Use these to personalize any letters you write and on receipts you give customers. Don't spend money having expensive stationery printed, but business cards would be nice.

2. A Price List

How do you know how much to charge? That's a hard question for every young entrepreneur. You want your price to be low enough that people will hire you, but high enough to be worth all the work.

Sometimes the customer will tell you how much they pay for a certain job. But most people will ask how much you charge. Talking to customers about your pay is easier when you have a price list. Spend some time listing the services or products your business sells and the prices.

To help decide how to set your prices, answer the following questions:

1. What do other people earn for the same work?

This calls for some research. Ask your friends how much they earn for doing the same job. Then find out how much adults are paid to do the job. The amount you charge should be fair when compared to the "going rate" in your area.

2. How hard is the work?

More difficult jobs will be worth higher pay. For example: You should expect to get paid more for mowing a yard with high grass (hard to do) than for watering house plants (easy to do).

3. How long will it take?

Washing driveways for $5 each might be good pay if the job takes less than two hours. To get a fair wage, you will have to charge more for longer jobs. Estimate how long the job will take. Then multiply the number of hours by what you feel is fair pay per hour. Once you make a deal, you must honor what you said even if the job takes longer.

4. How much experience do you have?

If you are just starting out, you may want to charge less or let the customer pay you what they think the job is worth. As you get experience, you will expect to get paid more, and you will be able to raise your prices.

5. How much will the supplies cost?

If you are providing the supplies for the job, your pay should be high enough to cover the expenses as well as pay you for working. If you are selling something, your prices have to be high enough to cover the cost of the product and pay you for your time.

Handling your money business successfully means having money left after you pay your expenses to make the job worth all your effort.

INCOME: Everything you get paid.

EXPENSES: Everything you spend to run your business.

PROFIT: The money you have left after you subtract your expenses from your income.

Estimating your income and expenses before you give a price on a job will help you set your prices high enough to make a profit. It can also help you avoid the mistake of starting a project that won't make enough money.

Before you accept a job, show the customer your price list and discuss your pay. Make sure you both agree on exactly what work is to be done and the amount you are to be paid. Customers will admire your business-like approach.

3. A Record-keeping System

Keeping good records is the only way to know how your money business is going.

You need a system for keeping track of every penny you earn and every penny you spend. Then you can tell how much profit your business is really making.

It doesn't have to be a fancy system. But every business transaction you make should have a piece of paper to explain it.

Here's what you need:

1. Two shoe boxes
2. Customer receipt forms
3. Purchase order slips
4. A spiral notebook
5. Large envelopes

· It may surprise you to know that many adult entrepreneurs use the "shoe box" system of record keeping. If you don't have shoe boxes, use small school supply boxes or large envelopes.

· On the next page is a sample customer receipt form. You can buy receipt books at office supply stores, make them on your computer, or photocopy our sample.

· The purchase order slips can be homemade. Just take some 3 x 5 cards or small slips of paper and write "Purchase Order" at the top.

· Save money on envelopes by reusing those you get in the mail.

CUSTOMER RECEIPT

BUSINESS NAME
ADDRESS
PHONE NUMBER

DATE:	NUMBER:
CUSTOMER:	
ADDRESS:	

FOR:	AMOUNT:
SUBTOTAL:	
TAX:	
TOTAL:	
PAID: RECEIVED BY:	

How to Run a "Shoe Box" Record-keeping System

1. Label one shoe box "INCOME" and the other "EXPENSES."

2. Each time you sell something or do a job, fill out a customer receipt. Use carbon paper to make two copies: one for your customer and one to put in your box marked "INCOME."

3. Each time you spend money on your business, save your store receipt. Then use a "purchase order" slip to record the date, how much you spent, and what you bought. Attach the store receipt to the purchase order and put it in the box marked "EXPENSES."

4. Open your spiral notebook to two facing pages. Label the left page "IN-COME" and the right page "EXPENSES." Use a ruler to make columns on each page like the samples below.

INCOME		
DATE	SOURCE	AMOUNT

EXPENSES		
DATE	ITEM	AMOUNT

5. Once a week, take all your receipts out of the INCOME box and list them in your notebook on the INCOME page for the month. Then take all your purchase orders and list them on the EXPENSE page for the month.

6. At the end of each month, total the INCOME page and the EXPENSE page. Make new pages for the next month. Store each month's receipts and purchase orders in a separate envelope.

7. You can total your income and expenses anytime during the month to see how your business is going. But at the end of each month, you should prepare a special report called a "profit and loss statement" (sometimes called a "P & L").

The formula for making a profit and loss statement is the same you've already been using: **income** minus **expenses** equals **profit.**

PROFIT & LOSS STATEMENT

FOR MONTH OF:

TOTAL INCOME: _____

TOTAL EXPENSES: _____

PROFIT (or loss): _____

You can make your P & L statement more detailed by listing where you got the money under INCOME and how you spent the money under EXPENSES. The P & L statement gives a short, one-page summary of your business transactions each month. Keep your monthly P & Ls and compare them to see how your business is changing.

Another Way to Look at Your Profits

Suppose you made $50 profit in June and $75 profit in July. You would say you made the most profit in July, right? Well, maybe. How many hours did you work to make those profits?

If you know how many hours you worked and how much you earned, you can figure how much you earned per hour. Use the formula below:

$$\text{Time} \overline{)\text{Profit}}^{\text{Hourly Wage}}$$

Let's say you worked 10 hours to make $50 in June. You earned $5 per hour. If you worked 20 hours to make $75 in July, you earned $3.75 per hour. Now which month was most profitable? The real story on your profits is the amount you made per hour.

To keep track of how much you are earning per hour, write the amount of time you worked on each project on the customer receipt. At the end of the month, add up your time and figure your hourly wage.

4. A Budget

At the end of Chapter 1, you were given a challenge to set some goals for your money business:

· How much money do you want to earn?
· How much will you save?
· How much will you spend?

Your answers to these questions will change from time to time, and your goals will change from time to time. But you should keep setting new goals and aiming at new targets *all of the time.*

When you write down exactly how much money you want to earn and how you want to spend it, you are starting a money plan. This money plan is often called a **budget.** Use the budget worksheet on the next page to make your money plans for the next month.

 It's easy to see that your income must be enough to cover your expenses. This is called "balancing" your budget. You've got to make sure your "OUT-go" matches your "IN-come." That's not easy.

What happens if the amount you plan to spend is more than your income? To solve that problem, you will have to **earn more** . . . or **spend less.**

If you have trouble balancing your budget (we all do), try listing the things you want or need in order of their importance. Then you will know which things you can take off the list or delay until you have more money.

BUDGET WORKSHEET

FOR MONTH OF: _____

LIST ALL POSSIBLE INCOME   AMOUNTS

    Allowance:

    Gifts:

    Oddjobs:

    Business income:

    Other income:

LIST ALL POSSIBLE EXPENSES   AMOUNTS

    Business needs:

    Something you want:

    Giving to help others:
    (Usually 10% of your income)
    Savings:
    Other:

TOTAL INCOME: _____ TOTAL EXPENSES: _____

Even when we set goals and make good plans, it sometimes seems as if money has wings. Where does it all go? How do you keep from blowing your savings before you reach your goal?

If you never seem to know where your money goes, try keeping a money diary for a few weeks. Every time you spend a penny, write it down in a notebook. Put the date, the amount, and what you bought. Then answer yes or no: Was this spending planned in my budget? You may be surprised at what you learn about your spending.

How to stay on your budget:

· *Picture your goal.* Keep thinking about that new skateboard. Put pictures of it on your wall or the bathroom mirror. Dream about it every day.

· *Put your money in the bank.* You won't be as tempted to spend the money if it's out of reach. Open a savings account and deposit your money each week. Remember, while your money is in there, it's earning *more* money — *interest!*

· *Track your savings with a chart.* Seeing that you are really making progress will help you keep going. Keep a chart in your notebook or make a poster for your room. Each time you save, color in a little more of the bar to show how much closer you are to the goal.

· *Stay out of the stores.* Don't go shopping unless it's for things planned in your budget. Ground yourself from video games for a while. Be willing to wait. The rewards are worth it.

5. A Schedule

As a busy student and young entrepreneur, you can see that managing time is important.

You need time to do the jobs you've promised your customers.

You also need time for school, family, and fun.

You even need time to just do *nothing!*

Three tools for managing time:

1. *A calendar:* Use the calendar pages in this book to keep track of your jobs and appointments.

2. *"To-do" lists:* Keep lists of things to do. Start out with a master list of everything to do for a week. Then make smaller lists for each day.

3. *A schedule:* When you have a lot to do, it helps to make daily schedules — much like the schedule you have at school for classes.

Use the chart on the next page to arrange your weekly schedule. First mark in times already taken for school, homework, music lessons, and social activities. Then schedule the times you can work on your business. If you have more to do than can fit in your schedule, make a list of the most important things to do. These are called your **priorities.** Successful people must set priorities — or make choices — about how they use both time and money.

WEEKLY TIME SCHEDULE

	MON	TUES	WED	THURS	FRI	SAT	SUN
7 AM							
8 AM							
9 AM							
10 AM							
11 AM							
NOON							
1 PM							
2 PM							
3 PM							
4 PM							
5 PM							
6 PM							
7 PM							
8 PM							
9 PM							
10 PM							

CHAPTER 4

SPRING MONEY-MAKING PROJECTS

Spring is the time of year for new beginnings. The fresh green leaves on the trees, the sunny days, and the warmer temperatures are a welcome change from the dreary, cold days of winter. For many people, spring is the time for opening the house, cleaning out the garage, and starting a garden. For the young entrepreneur, spring also brings new opportunities.

Tips on Spring Money-making Opportunities

· *It's time for spring clean-up and fix-up.* Expect to find opportunities like cleaning out garages, washing windows, or painting lawn furniture.

· *It's time for spring gardens.* You can earn money helping put in new flower beds, selling plants, growing herbs, and weeding gardens.

· *It's time for spring sports.* Baseball season is starting, so look for jobs helping with practice and equipment.

· *Spring holidays* are Easter, St. Patrick's Day, Mother's Day, and graduation. Start early planning gift items and holiday projects.

MARCH

GOAL #1: _____

SUNDAY	MONDAY	TUESDAY	WEDNESDAY

GOAL #2: _____

THURSDAY	FRIDAY	SATURDAY	NOTES

APRIL

GOAL #1: _____

SUNDAY	MONDAY	TUESDAY	WEDNESDAY

GOAL #2: _____

NOTES

THURSDAY	FRIDAY	SATURDAY

MAY

GOAL #1: _____

SUNDAY	MONDAY	TUESDAY	WEDNESDAY

GOAL #2: _____

NOTES

THURSDAY	FRIDAY	SATURDAY

TO-DO LIST

KID BIZ #1: CALL-A-KID!

It's spring and busy people in your neighborhood need help with all kinds of oddjobs. Kids in your neighborhood need ways to earn extra cash.

Why not match up the people who have jobs with the kids who need money?

How to get started: Pass out cards like this.

CALL-A-KID!

Need help getting things done?
PHONE ALLEN: (Your Phone)

Good Help — Any Job

On the lower part of the card or flyer, list the services you offer and the prices. You can start out doing all the work yourself. As your business grows, hire other kids.

Here's how it works:

1. Choose kids you can count on to do the work. Then spend your time getting customers.
2. Make your prices attractive. People will feel it's worth giving your business a try.
3. Keep a job schedule so customers can count on you to have someone there at the same time each week.
4. Each time you match a kid with a job, they pay you ten percent of the earnings.

This idea can stay small or grow as large as you wish. Starting in the spring will give you a head start toward growing larger this summer.

KID BIZ #2: CAR WASH AND WAX

Washing cars is a water-splashing, fun way to earn money when the weather turns warm this spring.

Almost every family in your neighborhood owns at least one car. And they *all* have to be washed — again and again! That's a lot of dirty cars! Why not cash in on all that dirt by starting your own car wash business?

Doing the job:

1. Use mild dishwashing liquid in a bucket of warm water. Wash the car in sections, using a soft rag or sponge. Rinse as you go to keep the soap from drying on the car.
2. Use a brush to scrub the tires and headlights.
3. After the car is clean, go back and wipe the windows with glass cleaner and paper towels.
4. To avoid water spots, wipe the car dry with old rags.
5. For a wax job, choose the best quality, easy-to-apply wax you can find. Follow the directions exactly.
6. Cleaning the inside of the car means to vacuum, clean the mats, wipe the dashboards, and clean the inside of the windows.

Setting prices: Make a price list for various wash and wax jobs. Include a higher price for vans and trucks. Your prices should cover all expenses, plus pay you for your effort.

KID BIZ #3: WASHING WINDOWS

Many people welcome spring with a good household cleaning. But window washing is one of the chores most folks love to forget.

There are lots of people with dirty windows in your neighborhood. . . . And they're just waiting for someone like you to save them from having to do the job!

Your window-washing service will get the dirty work done quickly and earn plenty of bucks.

How to get started:

1. Practice on your own windows at home until you develop a good system.
2. Make some flyers advertising your window-washing service.
3. Fix up a box or bucket to carry everything you need for the job.
4. Find customers by handing out flyers, asking people you know, and knocking on doors. Go dressed for work, and you may get hired on the spot!

Bonus ideas:

· Work with a partner, one person inside and the other outside. You can do twice as many jobs.

· Keep a list of your customers and call them in six months. Their windows will be dirty again!

KID BIZ #4: OUTDOOR PAINTING

Another profitable "spring thing" project is painting outdoor furniture, fences, dog houses, porches, decks, or storage sheds.

This kind of painting is not as difficult as house painting or indoor painting. And it's a good way to get experience with a paint brush.

How to get started:

1. Take a good look around your neighborhood. Make note of possible customers and projects.
2. Print some announcements of your painting service. Then visit each target customer on your list.
3. Make an agreement on the job to be done, the amount you will be paid, and who is to buy the supplies.

Painting tips:

- Wear old clothes, shoes, and hat.
- Keep all your paint rags, brushes, paint scraper, roller, and tools in one box or bucket.
- Protect the area where you work from drips and spills with newspaper or drop cloths.
- Remove loose paint, dirt, and grease before you paint.
- Paint from top to bottom.
- Clean up your mess and inspect your work before asking for your pay.

KID BIZ #5: GARAGE CLEANING

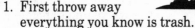

If you are really looking for a good way to earn money, try a garage cleaning service. Garages are not hard to keep orderly if they are cleaned once a month.

1. First throw away everything you know is trash.
2. Ask for a list of other things to throw away.
3. Then start sweeping the floor and organizing what's left.
4. Put things away in groups: things for the pool, things for the yard, things for painting, etc.
5. Ask customers to tell others about your work.

No matter how hard people try, garages get dirty, messy, and cluttered. If you are good at organizing things, make dirty garages your specialty.

KID BIZ #6: ASSISTANT GARDENER

People who enjoy gardening need extra help in the spring. They need an assistant gardener. That's you!

Ways you may help:

· Use a shovel or garden tiller to work the beds.
· Set landscaping timbers, bricks, or borders.
· Move shrubs.
· Spread mulch or bark chips.

53

KID BIZ #7: FIND-A-HOME
FOR PETS

Spring is a happy time of year when trees get green, flowers bloom, and little kittens and puppies are born. But many of these little pets will not survive unless homes are found for them.

A find-a-home service will help save these unwanted animals, and *feed your piggy bank!*

How to get started:

1. Watch for people who need help finding homes for kittens and puppies. People you know right now may need your service.
2. Watch for "Free Kitten" or "Free Puppy" signs. Busy people who are having trouble finding homes for their pets will be glad to pay you to do the job.
3. Decide what you will charge for your service. Check with pet stores to see what they charge, and make your price competitive.
4. Advertise your service with notices on bulletin boards in your neighborhood.

How to find homes for pets:

Weekends and holidays are the best times to give away or sell pets. Take the kittens or puppies to a busy location, such as in front of a grocery store. Put them in a box with an eye-catching sign. Then ask each person that goes by if they want a kitten or puppy. Before long, they will all have homes.

KID BIZ #8: GOLF CADDIE

Mild weather brings golfers out like "spring honey bees flocking to flowers." And it's time for *you* to be out, too!

You can earn fast cash on the golf course as a caddie.

Learning to caddie is not that hard. Your job is mostly to carry golf clubs and do things to help the golfer play well.

How to get started:

· Contact any golfers you know and tell them you want to become a caddie. Offer to caddie at a reduced pay so you can get experience.

· When you are on the golf course, watch what other caddies do. Then ask questions. You'll learn fast.

· When you are ready to hire out as a caddie, leave your name and phone number in the office at the golf course. Golfers will be calling you.

How much will you earn?

Well, that depends on you. Beginners start at $10, while experienced caddies may earn up to $1,000 in a pro golf tournament. Set a goal for what you want to earn as a caddie.

KID BIZ #9: PRACTICE PARTNER

Spring brings the beginning of baseball season. And ball-players who are serious about being good will start practicing.

But how can a baseball player practice hitting with no one to pitch and no one to field?

Serious athletes need help in order to put in extra practice. That means *cash opportunity* for you as a practice partner!

Here's what to do:

· Watch for an athlete practicing alone at a park, vacant lot, softball field, or school. Then ask if you can help by pitching.

· Take a few pitches to find out how the player wants the ball. You'll catch on quickly.

· After all the balls are hit, gather them quickly and be ready to pitch again.

· Ask the players you've worked for to tell others about you.

· Contact managers of local teams and tell them you want jobs. Develop a list of regular customers and contacts.

Bonus idea: Consider other sports. How about being a practice partner for tennis?

KID BIZ #10: EQUIPMENT MANAGER

All sports teams need someone to take care of the equipment and assist the coach.

How an equipment manager helps the team:

1. Keeps up with all the balls, bats, gloves, uniforms, masks — all the things the team needs.
2. Passes out the equipment before the game and takes it up afterwards.
3. Helps the players know whose turn it is to bat or go into the game.
4. Helps the coach keep records on the players.

How to get started:

- Look for places where teams are practicing. Ask the coaches if they need some help with equipment.
- Start out with Little League teams or other youth sports teams. You can get some experience as a volunteer or work for lower pay.
- City recreation programs, the YMCA, and high school teams may also need your help.
- Your experience may lead to a well-paying position with a professional team in the future. Learn all you can!

Bonus idea: You can also earn money in sports by training to be an umpire or game official.

KID BIZ #11: BIRTHDAY CLOWN

Help parents surprise those kids at the next birthday party!

Become a birthday clown! You can have fun and earn money at the same time with this plan.

Getting started:
1. Decide on a costume and makeup. Get ideas from magazines and books on clowning.
2. Work up some short clown routines that may include balloon tricks, magic, jokes, juggling, mime, gymnastic stunts, or dance. For extra help, take a class on clowning at your community center.
3. Pass out colorful and eye-catching flyers in your neighborhood. Don't forget that businesses, hospitals, and restaurants often hire clowns.
4. Appear as often as possible in costume!

Your job:
· Entertain guests.
· Lead games.
· Help with refreshments.
· Pose for pictures.
· Act a little silly.

Most of all, *have fun!* Everyone will love you!

Your pay: Before accepting the job, discuss your duties and your fees. You should earn $5 to $10 an hour at first, and more as you get experience. (Professional clowns earn $60 to $80 an hour.)

KID BIZ #12: WEEDING FLOWER BEDS

People who take a lot of pride in their spring gardening will be needing your help when the weeds start growing.

Weeds always grow faster!

Tips on weeding:

- For large gardens, use a sharp hoe.
- For flower beds, use a small trowel or weeding tool.
- Often the best way to get weeds out by the roots is to pull them by hand.
- Wear gloves. Hands and fingers are made to count money — not to dig!
- Be sure you know which are the weeds and which are the plants. Don't pull up the flowers by mistake.

KID BIZ #13: SELL BEDDING PLANTS

Selling starter plants is a very good way to earn money in the spring. Earn extra money by offering to set out the plants. People love to see their flower beds come alive after a long winter!

- Grow your own from seed in small cups of potting soil.
- Take cuttings from your own plants.
- Ask another gardener for thinnings.
- Buy wholesale from a nursery.

KID BIZ #14: RAISE PETS TO SELL

Kids who love animals will enjoy raising pets to sell. There are many animals you may choose to raise: birds, tropical fish, gerbils, rabbits, purebred cats and dogs, or even lizards.

Start with an animal you know about already.

· Pet stores will be glad to answer questions, help you get started, and may be a place to sell the animals you raise.
· Check with veterinarians for free booklets and information on the care of animals.
· Most important is to take care of your animals at all times. Keep them fed, healthy, and clean, and you will have beautiful pets that people will want to buy.

KID BIZ #15: BASEBALL CARDS

Is your hobby collecting baseball cards? Why not make it even more profitable?

· Buy cards at low wholesale prices through catalogs and magazine ads. Keep what you want and sell the rest to your friends. Since you can sell cards for less than local stores, you'll have plenty of customers . . . And money to buy more cards.

KID BIZ #16: USED BOOKS

People who like to read are always watching for bargains on used books and magazines.

Find ways to get used books free — or almost free — and you can make some money with a used book sale.

Scouts, church youth groups, or school clubs can use this idea to raise funds. The books will be donated by parents and friends.

USED
BOOK
SALE

Where to get books:
1. Get a bargain on leftovers from other book sales, garage sales, or library sales.
2. Ask people to give you books and magazines they don't want after spring cleaning.
3. Search your own house for books you are ready to sell.

Where can you sell books?
· Used books and magazines sell fast in garage sales.
· If you collect enough books, stage a giant used book sale.
· Flea market dealers and used book stores buy books and magazines by the box.

Never throw away a book! Donate what you don't sell to groups working for world literacy.

KID BIZ #17: EASTER BUNNY VISITS

Everybody loves the Easter Bunny. They'll love *you*, too, if you dress up like the Easter Bunny and visit the kids on Easter!

Getting started:

1. Start planning one month early.

2. Borrow, rent, or make a costume.

3. Advertise with flyers. Ask everyone who has small children.

4. Schedule the visits.

5. Call each customer back on the day before the visit.

Making visits:

· Allow about thirty minutes for each visit and at least thirty minutes between visits.
· Surprise the kids, deliver some good treats, and let the parents take plenty of pictures.
· Stick to your schedule and be on time.
· Most of all *have fun!* If you are having a good time, so will the kids.

More tips: Buy treats for the kids on sale. Try to find something a little different. Charge more for the time to visit parties. And remember, grocery stores and restaurants like the Easter Bunny too!

KID BIZ #18: EASTER BASKET TREATS

Here's an Easter treat children will love, and it's *sugar-free*. It's a plastic Easter egg with the child's name and a simple design painted on it.

If you start asking parents a few weeks before Easter, you can take orders for hundreds. Parents love to give treats that don't cause cavities.

Other ideas for Easter treats without sugar:

Pipe cleaner Easter bunnies, Easter chicks made of pom poms, finger puppets, and bean bag Easter eggs. Craft magazines will help you think of more ideas.

· Start making your sugar-free treats well before Easter. Things you can put kids' names on will sell best.

· Show samples of your creations to friends and neighbors and start taking orders.

· Increase profits by shopping for the best prices on supplies.

· Make a work schedule so you will have all orders filled before Easter.

KID BIZ #19: COMPUTER SERVICES

Do you enjoy computers? Why not cash in on your computer skills?

Use your computer to run your own business better. And use your computer to earn money. There are lots of services you can offer.

Things you can do on computer:

· Make custom greeting cards for Easter, St. Patrick's Day, Mother's Day, and graduation.

· Design party invitations, party banners, birthday cards, thank you notes, and birth announcements.

· Make signs for craft shows, garage sales, bake sales, and community events.

Tips for success:

1. Know your software and what it can do.
2. Design an attractive flyer to advertise.
3. Make samples of cards, flyers, and signs to show customers.
4. Offer a variety of colored papers.
5. Always keep back-up copies.

Computer services are in great demand today. Let people know about your skills.

KID BIZ #20: PLANT SALE

Spring is the perfect time for a giant plant sale. And this is a project that can be *pure profit*.

School, church, or scout groups may also find plant sales are good money-making projects.

Plant sales are profitable:

- Plants are expensive, so people love to buy where they get good bargains.

- Plant lovers can never resist buying a few more plants. You'll have several they can't live without!

- Most of the plants you sell will cost you nothing.

How to get free plants:

1. Ask your neighbors if you can help thin out their overcrowded flower beds. Your pay is all the plants they don't want.

2. Ask people who are redoing their landscaping if you can have plants they throw away.

3. Ask your parents about thinnings and cuttings from plants in your yard.

4. Don't forget house plants. Cuttings can be taken several weeks before your sale, rooted, and planted in paper cups. Ask people with lots of houseplants for clippings.

KID BIZ #21: FRESH HERBS

The latest news in great cooking today is fresh herbs. As the demand for fresh herbs has increased, herb growing has become a profitable business.

If you enjoy growing things, a small herb garden can be a perfect money-maker.

One starter plant costs about $0.69 and will take very little room to grow. The plants can be harvested again and again. Restaurants and catering services pay as much as $1 a stalk. Friends and neighbors will also want to buy your herbs.

KID BIZ #22: WILD BERRIES

If you've ever tasted a fresh berry pie, you know why people pick berries in the spring!

People who can't get out to the berry patch will buy all you can pick.

Tips for success:

- Start by scouting out prime berry-picking spots. Adults can give advice on what kinds grow in your area and when the season starts.

- Take orders from neighbors, relatives, and friends so you can pick and sell straight from the berry patch.

KID BIZ #23: PLASTIC BUCKETS

Look for someone with lots of work to do, and you'll find someone who needs a bucket!

People want buckets for car washing, gardening, fishing, carrying things, and countless household chores.

Yet hundreds of one-gallon, five-gallon, and ten-gallon buckets are thrown away every day. You can earn extra cash selling buckets you get for free.

Finding buckets:

1. Buckets are often thrown away by businesses. Check with paint stores, restaurants, and home repair businesses in your area.
2. Ask someone you know who works in a factory or refinery to save buckets for you.
3. If you find buckets with lids, sell the lids too.

Selling buckets:

1. Before selling, clean the buckets thoroughly.
2. Sell the buckets in your next garage sale.
3. Sell buckets from a sign in your yard.
4. Call hardware stores, bait and tackle shops, or nearby marinas. Offer to deliver ten to twenty buckets at a time. They will buy all you can bring. And it's all profit!

KID BIZ #24: BIKE REPAIRS

Sooner or later all bikes get "sick."

Tires go flat.
Spokes get loose.
Handlebars slip.
Seats wobble.
Chains come off.
Pedals break.

A sick bike means trouble for most people!

Start a repair service for all those broken down bikes and earn lots of spending money *fast!*

Steps to success:

1. Learn by practicing on your own bike, watching others, and asking lots of questions.
2. Gather the basic tools you'll need.
3. Tell people about your service. Put up some signs on bulletin boards.
4. Watch for kids with bike trouble and offer to help.
5. Offer a "Spring Tune-up" special for bikes that have been sitting in garages all winter.
6. Make a price list to help with quick estimates.
7. Keep some basic parts on hand such as bike tubes, master links, and spare pedals.

Bonus idea: Offer classes for kids on how to repair their own bikes.

KID BIZ #25: USED BIKES

When you see broken bikes or bike parts being thrown away, that's your clue for action!

Why? Flea market dealers, junk dealers, and people who rebuild bikes will buy the parts. But you can earn even more money on these parts.

There is a great demand for good used bikes. Why not build bikes from the old parts and sell them for $20 to $30 each?

Here's what to do:

· Start collecting old bike parts such as rims, good tires, seats, and pedals. If you have plenty of room for storage, save bike frames or whole bikes with good parts.

· The best way to learn how to build a bike is to work on old bikes you find. You can't hurt anything by trying. And bikes are fairly simple machines to work on.

· You will have buyers for most bikes before you get them finished. Signs on bulletin boards will bring even more customers.

Bonus idea: Let people know you also sell used bike parts. They will buy from you to save time and money on bike repairs.

✳ FOR MORE INFORMATION ✳

Cooperative Extension Service, University of (State), City, State, Zip. For more information about almost any subject in this book, write your state university extension service. Your librarian can help you find the complete address for your state.

Dollars & Sense Financial Camp, Smart Services, Inc., 255 Sunrise Ave., Suite 200, Palm Beach, FL 33480. Ask for information on weekend "camps" to learn about money, credit, and investing.

Home Office Computing Magazine, P.O. Box 51344, Boulder, CO 80321-1344. Beginners' information on how to use the computer in business.

Kids Mean Business, Homeland Publications, Dept. E-KB, 1808 Capri Ln., Seabrook, TX 77586. Ask for free sample of KIDS MEAN BUSINESS newsletter edited by *Kid Biz* authors Bonnie and Noel Drew. Provides the latest news on what kids all over the U.S. are doing to earn money.

National Association for the Self-Employed, 2328 Gravel Rd., Fort Worth, TX 76118. Ask for sample newsletter and information on scholarships.

Park Seed Co., P.O. Box 32, Greenwood, SC 29640. Ask for catalog to buy supplies for growing herbs.

Penny Power Magazine, P.O. Box 51777, Boulder, CO 80321-1777. Interesting reading for kids age eight to thirteen on how to use money wisely.

Small Business Administration (SBA). Call toll-free 1-800-368-5855. Give your area code and get the phone number of your local SBA office. Local offices will send free materials on starting a business.

✳ FOR FURTHER READING ✳

Babysitting for Fun and Profit by Rubie Saunders. Helpful advice on baby and childcare, how to get clients, and how to organize a summer play school. Archway Paperbacks, Simon & Schuster Inc., 200 Old Tappan Rd., Old Tappan, NJ 07675.

Be A Clown! by Turk Pipkin. The complete guide to instant clowning. Covers makeup, costumes, props, and tricks. Workman Publishing, 708 Broadway, New York, NY 10003.

Bicycle Maintenance and Repair by editors of ***Bicycling*** Magazine. A complete guide to thirty-seven common jobs on bikes. Rodale Press, 33 E. Minor St., Emmaus, PA 18098.

Pet Clean-up Made Easy by Don Aslett. How to clean up every kind of animal mess imaginable. Writer's Digest Books, 1507 Dana Ave., Cincinnati, OH 45207.

Speed Cleaning by Jeff Campbell and The Clean Team. A step-by-step system for cleaning the whole house. Dell Publishing, 666 Fifth Ave., New York, NY 10103.

Trash and Treasure: The Complete Book About Garage Sales by Jack and Chris Wilkie. How to turn unwanted belongings into cash. Bent Twig Publishing, 1088 Irvine Blvd., Suite 329F, Tustin, CA 92680.

Whatever Happened to Penny Candy? by Richard J. Maybury. Introduces young people to the principles of economics. Bluestocking Press, P.O. Box 1014, Dept. PCF, Placerville, CA 95667.

✓ ✓LAWNMOWER SAFETY

1. Know your equipment.

2. Keep children and pets away.

3. Wear sturdy work shoes.

4. Before mowing, inspect the yard. Pick up trash, rocks, wire, sticks, cans, and any other dangerous objects.

5. Never mow a wet lawn. Your feet are more likely to slip under the mower.

6. To unclog or adjust the mower, turn it off and wait for the blade to stop.

7. When using an electric mower, be careful not to run over the cord or entangle the cord.

8. Turn off and cool the mower before refueling. Refuel outside, not in the garage where gasoline vapors could be ignited by sparks from appliances.

9. Keep the mower in good repair.

10. Store mower and gasoline in a safe place away from smoking areas and small children.

CHAPTER 5

SUMMER MONEY-MAKING PROJECTS

School's out! Summer's here. It's time for lemonade stands, swimming pools, and picnics. When those hot, lazy days of summer get boring, it's the best time of the year for young entrepreneurs.

Tips on Summer Money-making Opportunities

· *It's time for vacations.* When your neighbors go out of town, earn money pet sitting, plant sitting, getting papers and mail, watering the yard, and filling in on paper routes.

· *It's time for summer yard work.* Grass needs to be cut at least once a week. Have you got a list of regular customers yet? Watch for extra jobs like trimming shrubs and cleaning driveways.

· *It's time for something unusual.* Try money-making projects like curb painting, pool cleaning, or a yard sale. Start a neighborhood newsletter or sell shell crafts.

· *Special days* are Father's Day and Fourth of July. Summer also means weddings and lots of people moving. There's plenty of opportunity for young entrepreneurs!

JUNE

GOAL #1: _____

SUNDAY	MONDAY	TUESDAY	WEDNESDAY

GOAL #2: _____			NOTES
THURSDAY	FRIDAY	SATURDAY	

JULY

GOAL #1: _____

SUNDAY	MONDAY	TUESDAY	WEDNESDAY

GOAL #2: _____			NOTES
THURSDAY	FRIDAY	SATURDAY	

77

AUGUST

GOAL #1: _____

SUNDAY	MONDAY	TUESDAY	WEDNESDAY

GOAL #2: _____   NOTES

THURSDAY	FRIDAY	SATURDAY

TO-DO LIST

KID BIZ #26: SELL SLUSH

Having a lemonade stand is as traditional as kids going barefoot in the summer. If you're ready for bigger things, try this new idea.

Use the recipe below to make homemade slush in your favorite flavors. It's so good, people will beg you to make some more!

What you need:

2 pkg. unsweetened drink mix
1 (48-oz.) can pineapple juice
2 cups of sugar
Water

How to make slush:

1. Mix the first three ingredients in a 1/2 gal. pitcher.
2. Add water to make a full 1/2 gal. of mix. Pour mix into a large bowl or pan.
3. Add another 1/2 gal. of water and stir well.
4. Set the mix in your freezer for three to four hours.
5. When the mix starts getting icy, stir every thirty minutes for three to four more hours.
6. You'll have 1 1/2 gal. of slush to sell, if you resist the temptation to sample!
7. Slush keeps well in an ice chest or cooler.

Selling slush:

· This drink is much like the slush people buy at convenience stores. Set your price lower, but high enough to make a good profit.
· Sell with a stand in front of your house, or use a wagon for a portable stand. Put a sign on the wagon and you can sell at the park or at your neighbor's garage sale. It won't last long on a hot summer day!

KID BIZ #27: CURB PAINTING

The amount of money you can earn painting house numbers on curbs in the summer is *unlimited!*

People like to have their house number on the curb because it makes it easier for fire, police, or ambulance calls to be answered.

It also helps friends and pizza deliveries to find the right house!

Here's how to get ready:

1. Buy three sets of three-inch stencils from an office supply store so you have enough numbers.
2. Gather other supplies: two plastic spines from clear report covers, stiff brush, spray paint, and poster board. Fix a box to carry things.
3. Practice on cardboard boxes until you can make the numbers neat and readable.

Doing the job:

1. Brush loose dirt off the curb.
2. Using a rectangle cut in the posterboard as a pattern, spray the background white.
3. Insert the numbers in the plastic spine to hold them while you paint.
4. Center the numbers over the background. Tape them down and spray the numbers black. Carefully remove the stencils.
5. Charge $2–$4 a job. Many kids earn $50 a day!

KID BIZ #28: BABYSITTING FOR GROUPS

Here's how to multiply your earnings as a babysitter this summer: You and a friend can earn twice your normal hourly pay when you babysit for mothers' groups.

Getting jobs:

1. Watch the newspaper and bulletin boards for news of women's exercise classes or club meetings.
2. Call and ask if they will be needing a sitter.
3. Get someone you know who attends a class to recommend you and your partner for the job.

Tips for success:

· Always have a partner to work with.
· Arrive fifteen to thirty minutes early to get ready.
· Plan games, stories, and play activities.
· Let older children be helpers with the younger children.
· Don't disturb the mothers unless there is an emergency.
· Distract an unhappy child with play.
· For long meetings, plan snacks and perhaps a craft time. Kids will love it.
· Have the room cleaned up and the kids ready to go when the mothers are ready.

Bonus idea: You may get some bonus jobs from the mothers if you let them know you are available. Give out cards with your name and phone number when mothers pick up the children.

KID BIZ #29: ERRAND SERVICE

One thing you have during the summer that parents and businesspeople *don't* have is extra *time*. To save people time, start a general errand service.

Kinds of errands:

* Shopping
* Errands
* Deliveries

· Errands for neighbors may be returning a book to the library, getting gas for the lawnmower, buying groceries, or going to the cleaners.

· Errands for businesspeople may be picking up office supplies, delivering packages, getting something for lunch, or running to the post office.

Steps to success:

1. Make some cards or flyers to announce your errand service. Pass them out in your neighborhood and to local businesses.
2. Make personal calls to businesspeople. They will be regular customers with many errands.
3. Use your bike for transportation. If you don't have a basket, use a backpack.
4. Be sure you understand instructions. Write down addresses and lists of things to get.
5. Do the errand quickly and come straight back. Be careful to deliver all items in good shape and return any change.

Small jobs can add up to big bucks. Be dependable and you will have lots of regular customers.

KID BIZ #30: BOAT CLEANUP

If you live near water, fishing and boating are favorite summer recreations. A boat cleanup service is ideal for you.

Getting started:

- Give out flyers where you see a boat in the yard or driveway.
- Leave flyers at marinas, fishing piers, and bait shops.
- Ask a boat dealer about cleaning the boats on display once a week. It's easy cleanup, good pay, and steady work.

Doing the job:

1. Before you start, the front of the boat should be propped up and the drain plug open.
2. Remove all loose gear. Sweep up and remove any trash or leaves.
3. Scrub the boat inside and out with mild soap in a bucket of water. Work in sections and rinse before the soap dries.
4. To wax, use any good commercial boat wax and follow instructions exactly.
5. Return the gear to the boat when finished.

Bonus ideas: Additional earnings can come from cleaning boats with cabins or large boats docked in yacht basins. Another service you can offer is cleaning RVs. The pay for all of these services is excellent if you do good work.

KID BIZ #31: SHELL CRAFTS

People all over the world love the beauty of sea shells. They are used to decorate homes, make jewelry, and collect as hobbies.

You can make money selling shells you find along the beaches. People will pay high prices for shells you get free!

Shelling tips:

1. Go shell hunting two to four hours after high tide or after a storm tide. If you are the first one there, you may discover a treasure.
2. Clean most shells by soaking in a bucket of water and several cups of bleach.
3. Scrub shells with a soft brush and leave outside to air and cure.
4. Rub smooth shells with mineral oil to make them shine. Or paint with a thin coat of shellac.

Selling shells:

- Gift shops, craft stores, and shell shops will buy shells and driftwood.
- Shells sell fast at garage sales.
- Craft items made with shells are very popular gifts to sell. Have fun creating shell pictures, decorated mirrors, funny animals, jewelry, planters, decorated boxes, and baskets.

You can do shell crafts even if you can't collect your own. Just order your shells from wholesalers.

KID BIZ #32: HELP PEOPLE MOVE

Whenever you see a neighbor moving, you are looking at a way to earn money!

Lots of people move in the summer and they *always* need more help! Watch for moving vans or trucks in your neighborhood.

Steps to success:

- Introduce yourself and offer to help.
- Check with your parents. NEVER go anywhere with people unless you have permission.
- Work quickly, but be careful not to damage anything. Watch for extra ways to help.

KID BIZ #33: GET PAPERS AND MAIL

GOING OUT OF TOWN?

Let Andy take care of your papers and mail!

When your neighbors go out of town, they need someone to take care of their papers and mail.

Think about it: If this job takes ten minutes and you earn $1 a day, you are earning the same as $6 an hour! That's GOOD PAY.

KID BIZ #34: PET SITTING

People who have pets need someone dependable to care for their animals when they go on vacation this summer. If you enjoy animals, you'll like this job.

How to get started:

1. Tell friends, relatives, and neighbors about your pet-sitting service. Pass out flyers.
2. Before accepting jobs, visit the home to meet the pet. If the animal seems hard to manage, don't take the job.
3. Discuss your pay and make a list of all instructions.
4. Ask the owners how to contact them in an emergency.

Success tips: Move slowly around a new animal until he knows you are a friend. Be careful when going in and out. Clean up any mess the pet makes. If you have a problem, tell your parents.

KID BIZ #35: PET GROOMING

In the summer, pets need extra care and grooming. It's a good time for a pet grooming service.

Advertise that you give baths, give flea treatments, walk animals, and teach tricks.

PET GROOMING

Call 932-6754

(Continued)

Pet grooming tips:

- A veterinarian can tell you good flea products to use on animals. Ask for free booklets on care and grooming also.
- Put flyers out in your neighborhood, on bulletin boards, and at your vet's office.
- You can make a good income from pet grooming with a list of regular customers.

KID BIZ #36: PLANT-SITTING

When people are going out of town for a week or more, they need a sitter for their plants.

You can cash in on this money-making opportunity.

Plant-sitting tips:

- Learn all you can about house plants. Read, ask questions, and watch other people. Try growing a few plants of your own for experience.

- Start looking for customers by asking friends, relatives, and neighbors. Announce your service by passing out flyers.

- Before accepting a job, visit the home and get a detailed list of instructions.

- If you have problems with a plant, call your local nursery or garden shop for advice.

What a relaxing and enjoyable way to earn money!

KID BIZ #37: MOWING YARDS

Mowing yards is one of the most common ways kids earn their spending money in the summer. In fact, this job is the first thing most kids think of when they need fast cash. And it's still one of the best paying businesses a kid can have!

YOU GROW IT!
WE MOW IT!

TOM'S MOWING SERVICE
Call 973-2343

Advertise your business with a catchy slogan and bright colored paper. People will remember you!

Steps to success:
- When you get a yard, do the job right away.
- Mow neatly, blowing clippings away from walks and driveways. Always sweep.
- Remember the best way to get *more* jobs is to do a *good* job. Work on building a list of regular customers.
- Keep a schedule of your jobs and be dependable about going back at the same time each week.
- Look for extra jobs to do, such as weeding flower beds or raking.
- Don't forget about business property. These jobs are usually bigger and pay more.

Most kids start a yard business with borrowed equipment from home. You can buy your own mower and tools as your business grows.

KID BIZ #38: EDGE AND TRIM

Here's another hot tip to increase your lawn service business. Look for yards that are mowed but need edging and trimming.

There are always extra ways like this to earn money where you live. Make a practice of noticing jobs that are left undone. These are your hot opportunities!

Ideas for success:

· When you see a yard that needs your "edge and trim" service, knock on the door and ask about the job.

· Have flyers and business cards printed for advertising. Carry business cards with you and give them out — on the spot — when you see an opportunity.

· Team up with a friend who has a mower only. Your friend can mow, and you can edge and trim. You'll both get more jobs by offering better service.

· Don't forget townhomes and small businesses that have very little grass. A trimmer can do the whole job.

Safety tips: Wear sturdy shoes, long pants, and long sleeves. Use safety glasses, and know how to operate your equipment properly.

KID BIZ #39: WATERING SERVICE

See those folks spending a lot of time — and *money* — on their yards and outdoor plants? They will need someone to water for them if they go on vacation this summer.

These people could be *your* customers!

Remember the people in your neighborhood who have beautiful yards and plants. Ask these folks if you can water their yards when they are out of town. Leave your name and phone number so they can call you.

Ideas for success:

· Be sure you get complete instructions on the job. Write lists.
· Find out where the hoses, sprinklers, and any other equipment will be stored.
· Ask if there are other jobs you can do to help while they are gone.

Bonus ideas: Offer to feed the dog, get mail and papers, mow the yard, and check on the house. Extra jobs can add up to big bucks!

KID BIZ #40: PAPER ROUTE FILL-IN

Why do so many young
people — and adults — have
jobs delivering papers?

Because it's a good way to earn extra money!

Being a fill-in on a paper route is a good way to pocket
some of the paper delivery money, without the responsibility of
a full-time route. You can take as many or as few jobs as you
wish.

Steps to success:

- Ask friends with paper routes if you can fill in for them
  when they go on vacation this summer.

- Call the circulation departments of local newspapers. Ask
  to be on the list of fill-ins.

- Before you start a job, go on the route with the regular delivery person. Learn the list well before you try it on your
  own.

- Be dependable to throw the papers on time. Don't miss
  any addresses. You'll get lots more jobs.

KID BIZ #41: POOL CLEANING

Owning a pool is great, but there's plenty of work for the owner. Pools have to be taken care of and cleaned at least once a week.

If you want to earn some big bucks this summer, start a pool-cleaning service.

How to get started:

· If you don't own a pool, learn to do pool maintenance by working with a friend who does.
· Get customers by giving out flyers, asking people who have pools, or putting small ads in the newspaper.
· Before accepting a job, visit the home to see the pool, get instructions, and discuss how you will be paid.
· Your goal should be to get a list of regular customers. Then keep a schedule and do each job at the same time each week.
· Be dependable and your happy customers will tell others about you.

Pool cleaning steps:

1. Test the water.
2. Add the chemicals.
3. Vacuum the pool with proper equipment.
4. Use a deep net to clean floating trash.
5. Use a skimmer net to clean the top of the water.
6. Check and clean the filter. Then backwash.
7. Brush floor and sides of the pool.

KID BIZ #42: DRIVEWAY CLEANING

Here's another household problem that makes people crazy . . .

 . . . Cleaning the driveway! Getting up those oil spots! Scraping off the bubble gum! Pulling weeds that grow in the cracks!

You'll save a lot of folks from insanity if you start a driveway cleaning service.

How to get started:

1. Visit a hardware store and buy a good, strong cleaning product that will clean driveways.
2. Use a stiff brush and a good broom. Practice on your driveway at home.
3. Dress for work and go down the street knocking on doors. Watch for driveways that need sweeping or cleaning. Ask for the job.
4. If no one is home, leave a flyer on the door so they can call you.
5. Put more flyers on bulletin boards too. Check every few days. If your flyers are gone, put out some more.

You can become a driveway "specialist." Learn to be good at what you do, and you'll have lots of jobs.

KID BIZ #43: PAINTER'S HELPER

Painting the outside of a house is a *big job*. It's a project that takes several days — sometimes a week — and people always need help.

Keep your eye out this summer for neighbors who are painting. Offer to help and you'll earn fast cash.

Ways you can help:

Holding ladders and carrying supplies.
Handing tools, paint, rags to the painter.
Scraping, sanding, painting easy parts.
Cleaning brushes, rollers, and pans.
Cleaning paint drips on windows.
Bringing cold drinks — just being company.

Steps to success:

· Wear old clothes and a hat.
· Be alert and listen for instructions.
· Charge less until you get experience.
· Watch and learn about painting houses.

Bonus idea:

The skills you learn as a painter's helper will prepare you for earning extra money in the future. Painting houses can be a good paying part-time job when you go to college. Learn all you can.

KID BIZ #44: SHRUB AND TREE TRIMMING

Summer sunshine and rain makes trees, shrubs, and hedges grow extremely fast. They will need trimming about once a month.

This is a job people often pay someone else to do. Why not let them pay *you?*

GEORGE'S TRIMMING SERVICE
Call: 499-2326

Two ways to trim:

1. Look at the natural shape of the tree or shrub and give it a nice, even trim.
2. Choose a shape for the tree or shrub — a circle, or an oval, or flat on top and trim it to that shape. Check with the customer first

Tools to use:

- Hedge clippers — for shaping shrubs and hedges.
- Pruning shears — for cutting thicker branches that hedge clippers won't cut.
- Small saw — for removing small limbs.
- A shovel — for digging up entire shrubs.

Tip: Before you begin, ask the customer to tell you how much to cut and the shape they want. Remember to trim lightly. You can't put it back! But you can always trim more if it's not enough.

KID BIZ #45: NEIGHBORHOOD NEWSLETTER

Interesting things happen in your neighborhood all the time. Do you ever read about it in the paper? I doubt it! Your neighbors would enjoy a newsletter that tells about their babies, their parties, their ball teams, and their friends.

It doesn't have to be a fancy newsletter — just a page or two. You can type it, do it on computer, or hand-letter it. The news is what counts.

Look around your neighborhood. You will find lots to write about: pets, vacations, weddings, new neighbors, unusual ways to do things, school news, what folks say about world events, the award Johnny got in piano, and how Ann won a bicycle last week.

How to get started:

1. Gather news, make news, *find* news. There's news out there.
2. Write all about it. Then get it printed at a copy shop or Mom or Dad's work (with permission).
3. A business may print the newsletter for free if you let them advertise.
4. Sell the newsletter door-to-door or in front of the nearest grocery store. Be sure to sell one to everyone you wrote about too.
5. Keep your note pad handy. People will tell you more stories to put in next month's letter!

KID BIZ #46: CLEAN RENTAL PROPERTY

This guy owns a lot of rental property. He's a busy man! He's too busy to spend time cleaning houses or apartments when people move out.

If there is rental property in your neighborhood, help busy managers by starting a cleaning service.

How to get started:

- Watch for vacant houses or apartments with "For Rent" signs. Call the number on the sign and offer your rental property cleaning service.
- Look in the phone book under "Realtors." Call or mail flyers about your service to local real estate offices.
- After you have done a few jobs, ask for a letter telling about your work. Use the letter to show others you have experience and do good work.

How to do the job:

- Give the whole place a good, complete cleaning as you would your own house. This includes sweeping, mopping, washing walls, carrying off trash, perhaps some yard work. Owners want the house fresh and clean so new people will want to live there.
- Cleaning rental property is easy in one way. The rooms are empty. You don't have to move furniture or walk around things. Try it.

KID BIZ #47: YARD SALE

People throw away all kinds of good stuff when they move, clean the attic, or redecorate the house: dishes, picture frames, flower arrangements, Christmas decorations, drapes, lamps, small appliances, and even furniture.

You can make money recycling these usable discards.

Have a yard sale:

1. Ask friends and relatives to give you their throwaways for your yard sale.
2. Look around your house for things you haven't used in a long time.
3. Then set a date and advertise your sale. Make lots of signs so people can find your house.
4. If you want to have more fun and a really *big* sale, invite a few friends to bring their old junk and sell too!

KID BIZ #48: USED TOY SALE

How many toys, games, and books do you have in your room that you haven't touched in six months?

Kids outgrow toys almost as fast as they outgrow clothes! Summer is a great time to clean out your room and have a used toy sale.

How to get toys to sell: Get your friends together and go through each other's rooms looking for things to sell. Fix broken toys or invent new ones with the parts. Ask your relatives too.   (Continued)

Why people want used toys:

· New toys are expensive. Parents like to get bargains now and then.
· Kids don't mind if toys are a little used. They just like something different to play with.
· Day-care centers and church nurseries buy used toys to replace the ones they wear out so often.

Toy sale success: Toy sales can be as simple as setting up a small stand on your driveway. Or they can be giant-size events as large as a garage sale. Kids won't care how big or small the sale. They'll be there as soon as you put up the first sign!

KID BIZ #49: RE-SELL USED CLOTHING

While you're cleaning out your closets this summer, take a good look at all those clothes.

What do you do with clothes you've outgrown or gotten tired of? You turn them into *cash!*

A good place to sell your used clothing is a resale shop.

Here's how it works: Resale shops sell good used clothing they get from people (like you) who want to "re-sell" things. When you bring in clothes, you get an account number. Then when your items sell, they pay you 1/3 to 1/2 of the price. You will get a check in the mail once a month from the resale shop. Kids' clothes sell fast at the end of summer when school is starting. So *get busy!*

101

KID BIZ #50: WORMS & CRICKETS

If you live near some good fishing spots, make money this summer selling worms and crickets for bait.

The worms may object . . . but the fisherman will love you!

Friends and neighbors that like to fish will become your regular customers.

How to get worms:

1. Dig for worms beneath moist hay, leaves, or rotted wood — or in garden spots that have been mulched and kept moist.
2. Start a worm farm in your back yard. Buy starters from worm growers. They will give you free information on how to get started.

How to get crickets:

1. Clean and smooth an area about 18' x 36' near weeds and grass.
2. Sprinkle with cornmeal, cover with a burlap bag, and moisten.
3. After two days, harvest the crickets: Put a white cardboard "fence" around the area. Then shake the burlap bag and catch the crickets.

Bonus idea: Sell your worms and crickets to bait shops and fishing camps too.

KID BIZ #51: LIVE MINNOWS

When people are ready to fish — they need bait *now!*

Because summer is the prime fishing season, bait shops often run low on supplies. You can trap minnows to supply bait shops or to sell straight to your own customers.

How to get minnows:

1. Catch saltwater minnows in minnow traps baited with canned dog food or crushed crabs. Put your traps out in shallow, marshy areas along the shoreline near rocks or tall grass. If you don't get any in thirty minutes, move to another place.

2. Catch freshwater minnows with a net or seine. You'll find them in shallow water near weeds in small creeks or streams.

Selling tips:

· Keep your minnows alive in a bait bucket if you plan to sell them immediately.
· To keep minnows alive longer, you'll need a live well with an aerator.
· Signs on bulletin boards or on the roads near fishing areas will bring you plenty of local fishermen for customers.
· If you plan to sell to bait shops, call first and make an agreement on what they pay and how many they will buy.

KID BIZ #52: OUTDOOR HOUSE CLEANING

Cleaning mildew and algae off the outside of the house is another summer chore for many families.

Busy people often hire someone for this job. This is a good opportunity for you to earn extra money.

Steps to success:

· Make flyers announcing your service. Go through your neighborhood and leave the flyers at houses with mildew and algae on the outside.

· Gather your supplies: a stiff scrub brush, a good broom, a bucket, and bleach.

· Dress for work, carry your supplies, and go knock on a few doors. Tell people about your service and ask for the job.

· Show how you can improve the looks of their home by demonstrating. (Scrub a small area with a mixture of water and bleach.)

· Agree on the pay, who buys supplies, and special instructions before you start working.

· Wear rubber gloves, old clothes, and keep the bleach off *you*. Also, keep the bleach off grass and plants.

· Older teens may earn more by renting a pressure washer for these jobs.

CHAPTER 6

FALL MONEY-MAKING PROJECTS

Fall. Leaves crunching underfoot. Chilly mornings. A new school year. Football games. Pumpkins. Holiday decorations in the stores. Bake sales. Craft fairs. People thinking about their Christmas lists. All these are signs of money-making opportunity for the young entrepreneur.

Tips on Fall Money-making Opportunities

· *It's time to go back to school.* Now you can start all your school-based money-making projects. Sell school supplies, T-shirts in school colors, football spirit items, or handy snack foods. You have a whole school full of customers!

· *It's time to rake leaves.* You won't have many yards to mow in the fall, but you can make plenty of money raking leaves.

· *It's time for celebrating.* Expect to find opportunities to help build floats for parades, work at fairs, or help people entertain.

· *Fall holidays* are Halloween and Thanksgiving. Christmas shopping gets serious in November, so get your craft and gift items ready.

SEPTEMBER

GOAL #1: _____

SUNDAY	MONDAY	TUESDAY	WEDNESDAY

GOAL #2: _____			NOTES
THURSDAY	FRIDAY	SATURDAY	

OCTOBER

GOAL #1: _____

SUNDAY	MONDAY	TUESDAY	WEDNESDAY

GOAL #2: _____			NOTES
THURSDAY	FRIDAY	SATURDAY	

NOVEMBER

GOAL #1: _____

SUNDAY	MONDAY	TUESDAY	WEDNESDAY

GOAL #2: _____			NOTES
THURSDAY	FRIDAY	SATURDAY	

TO-DO LIST

KID BIZ #53: SCHOOL SPIRIT

One of the fun things about going back to school in the fall is the beginning of football season. It's time to wear school colors, yell your lungs out, and get into *school spirit!*

When football fever is high, students will buy *anything* that promotes the team. This is a kid biz opportunity . . . *for sure.*

And you're with your customers all day long . . . five days a week!

Things you might sell:

Anything with school colors or the team name: stickers, pens, pencils, book marks, tote bags, hair ribbons, socks, calendars, note pads, posters, rulers, giant paper clips, self-stick notes, and *more.*

How to get started:

1. Start out with a school spirit item that you can make at home with low-cost supplies. Craft stores are good places to get ideas.
2. Look under "advertising specialties" in your phone book. These businesses can supply almost any school spirit item you want. Ask them to send you a catalog.
3. Take a few samples of your product to school and start taking orders. (Be sure you stay "legal" according to school rules.)
4. As your school spirit business catches on, watch for new trends and add new products.

KID BIZ #54: SCHOOL SUPPLIES

What happens when teachers say, "Don't forget"? Kids forget folders, rulers, notebooks, pens — all kinds of supplies.

Why not make your backpack a mobile school store! Buy extra supplies and sell them to kids who forget (or run out).

How to get started:

· Do some research to find the best prices on common school supplies.
· Start with one or two most often needed items.
· Set your prices to give you at least 20% profit, and sell at the same price to everybody.
· As your business grows, you may increase your profit by purchasing supplies in bulk or when they are on sale.
· Never spend all your profits. Save some to invest back into the business if you discover a hot new item.
· Keep your business within school rules, or you will soon be *out* of business.

Bonus ideas:

1. Other useful items that students might buy are typing supplies, organizers, calculators, art supplies, or grooming necessities.
2. Get elementary school supply lists before school starts and assemble complete school supply sets. Sell door-to-door or take orders. Parents will like your time-saving idea!

KID BIZ #55: DESIGNER T-SHIRTS

They're a little crazy, always fun, and sometimes even artistic.

What are we talking about? T-SHIRTS! People love them! And they're a profitable business for today's young designer.

Wear your special T-shirt creations to school and everyone will want one!

How to get started:

1. Visit a craft store to learn about fabric paints and T-shirt supplies you will need.
2. Experiment with designs on old T-shirts and start developing your "style."
3. Once you hit on a unique idea, make a sample shirt and wear it to school.
4. When people ask you to make a T-shirt, quote a fixed price. You should get at least $5 to $10 for labor.
5. To keep from having to invest in blank T-shirts, have your customer supply the shirt. They should prewash the shirt, also.
6. As you get some money to invest, try making shirts to sell at a craft show or door-to-door.
7. You may also find a small shop in your town that will display the shirts and sell them in return for a percentage of the sales price.

Bonus idea: Make T-shirts for sports teams, scout groups, employee clubs, or special events.

KID BIZ #56: PUMPKIN PARTY

Kids want to do something fun on Halloween. Parents worry about safety. What to do?

Here's your answer. Begin a new tradition. Have a giant PUMPKIN PARTY for the kids in your community.

Wear a pumpkin costume, carry a few treats, and sell tickets door-to-door two Saturdays before Halloween.

Party ideas:

1. Tell kids to wear costumes and bring a sack of good treats to share at the end.
2. Have a costume contest. Give prizes for the Funniest, Weirdest, Most Original, Best Character. Don't encourage scary costumes.
3. A pumpkin-carving contest will add to the atmosphere. The carving is done at home and entries are judged at the party. Get local businesses to donate prizes.
4. Have some "old-fashioned" games. Outdoor games might be apple bobbing, a sock throwing contest, and marshmallow on a string.
5. Indoor games are quieter. Plan games for all ages. Older kids will like to help run them.
6. Give candy and small treats as game prizes. Serve other refreshments like popcorn and orange slush (see Kid Biz #26 for recipe).
7. End the party with a Pumpkin Parade. As the kids march to music, give out the treats they brought to share.

Everyone goes home with a bag full of goodies!

(Continued)

Pumpkin party success tips:

· If you plan a large party, get some friends to work with you.
· Start planning six weeks in advance.
· Research a location with more room, such as a church or community center.
· Arrange donations from businesses early. Then list them on your flyers.
· Use flyers generously all over the community. Give a phone number for more information.
· Notify local papers. What you are planning will make a good story!

KID BIZ #57: CANDY

Everyone loves candy all year round. But the fall holidays make "sweet treats" a profitable business!

What to sell:

· Candy you buy on sale.

· Candy you buy in large boxes or bags and divide up.

· Fancy candies or suckers you make with molds or kits from a craft shop.

· Homemade fudge — Use the no-fail recipe on jars of marshmallow cream.

Where to sell: School lunch periods, football games, church bazaars, and fall festivals.

KID BIZ #58: COOKIES

COOKIES! Chocolate Chip, Toll House, Peanut Butter, Oatmeal . . .

Everyone loves cookies! Cookies for school, cookies for church bake sales, cookies for the scout meeting, and don't forget some for the PTA.

Who bakes all those cookies? Busy families don't have time anymore! They need someone like you to start a cookie baking service. You can earn money just for knowing how to bake cookies!

Getting started:

1. Decide on two kinds of cookies — your favorites.

2. Figure exactly how much it costs to bake each recipe, then how much each cookie costs.

3. Set your prices high enough to make a profit, but low enough to be a good deal.

4. Make some flyers to announce your service. Give them to people you know and put them on local bulletin boards.

5. Take orders. Watch for school or community events. Call busy neighbors and offer to do their baking.

6. Change your selections and your flyers at each holiday. Do something special and unique.

(Continued)

Cookies made Mrs. Fields famous. She started in her own home and specialized in what she did best. Take a tip and be the BEST.

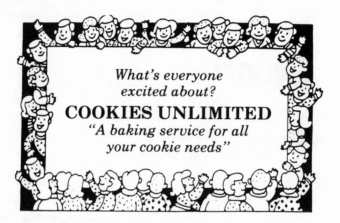

What's everyone excited about?

COOKIES UNLIMITED

"A baking service for all your cookie needs"

Steps to success:

· Take advantage of sales to get supplies at lowest prices. Watch for places to buy in bulk.

· Make arrangements with your family about using the kitchen and storing supplies. Keep promises!

· Test new recipes before you offer them to the public. Watch for new ideas.

· Take a class in cake decorating. Then offer fancy decorated cookies at a higher price.

· Be careful. Burnt cookies are *your* loss, not the customer's.

· Save time by baking several batches in one baking session. Keep some cookies in your freezer for rush orders.

· Develop a reputation for being dependable.

KID BIZ #59: FADS

If it's the latest, the newest, the most popular, what's "in," or cool — kids spend money on it!

Fads can make you money too! Watch for good buys on things everyone wants or collects. Then buy extras and sell to friends at school.

Fad ideas:

Some examples of fads are buttons, stickers, charms, and wild shoelaces. More recent fads are cool sunglasses, vests, "scrunchies" (fabric ponytail holders), friendship bracelets, dinosaurs, and Ninja turtles. If there's no fad, *start your own!*

KID BIZ #60: STUFFED TOYS

Soft, cuddly stuffed animals, toys, and dolls never go out of style. They're great gifts and sell quickly.

Easy to make: Draw your shape on paper. Cut it out and use it as a pattern to cut the fabric. Put the front and back together. Sew up the sides and leave a hole to stuff. Stuff, sew up the hole, and trim.

Fun to create: Visit toy stores and gift shops for ideas. Try clowns, teddy bears, funny monsters, and school mascots. Use materials you find at home — scrap fabric, bits of trim, sequins, buttons.

KID BIZ #61: ADOPT A GRANDPARENT

Older people often have problems getting chores done around the house and yard. Taking heavy trash to the curb, getting things out of the attic, and sweeping the drive-way are examples.

ANNOUNCING
★★★★★★★
Special Helpers
for
Senior Citizens

You could be a real help by starting a service for senior citizens called "Adopt-a-Grandparent."

Here's how it works:

- Since most older people can't afford to pay adult wages for simple chores, they will be glad to use your "adoption" service.

- Make flyers advertising your plan and suggested chores you are available to do.

- Make an agreement with your new "grandparent" about the job and the pay before you start.

- Schedule times for visits and be dependable.

- Take time to make friends with your adopted grandparent.

You'll get more for your service than just money. Senior citizens are full of wonderful stories and helpful information. They are great listeners when you have a problem — and very generous with cookies!

KID BIZ #62: PARADE FLOATS

Everyone loves a parade! The bands, the floats, the clowns, the firemen who throw candy — most of all, the excitement!

But a parade takes hours of planning and work for those who want to be in it.

You can earn some fast cash helping build those floats a few days before the parade. The next time there's a parade in your town, contact community organizations and businesses and ask for the job.

KID BIZ #63: FAIR BOOTHS

When there's a festival, craft show, or fair coming up, you should be thinking of people who will need extra help.

Artists and crafts people with booths will need you to help set up, run errands, wait on customers, and clean up.

How to get the job: Watch for announcements of local fairs. Contact small shop owners, artists, and crafts people to offer help. Or just go to the fair. You may find tired workers who need a break.

KID BIZ #64: HORSES

Fall makes people think of rodeos, horses, and Go Western Days. If you're a horse-lover, here's a money-making idea just for you.

People who have horses will hire you to clean tack and do grooming. You can get paid for doing something you already enjoy — working with horses. Be ready to work extra during rodeos, shows, and special events. There may also be a job for you at a local stable. Tell them you want to clean stalls, feed and exercise horses, and help around the stable.

KID BIZ #65: REFRESHMENT STANDS

As kids' sports have gotten *bigger,* parents have become *busier!* Parents are asked to help with the team, keep up the fields, and sell refreshments.

You can earn some extra cash by working in the refreshment stand for parents who are too busy to take their turn.

Leave your name with the manager of the stand. Or contact "team moms" so they can tell people you are available. Enjoy the game and get paid too!

KID BIZ #66: PARTY SERVICE

Everyone likes to be invited to a party! Here's your invitation to make money with a party service business. You can offer help with everything from the planning to the cleaning up.

Party services may include:

1. Shopping for a list of party supplies.
2. Cleaning and decorating the house.
3. Preparing food.
4. Serving food, getting ice, refilling the punch bowl, picking up empty plates, and washing dishes. Leave the hosts free to enjoy their guests.
5. Afterwards, clean the kitchen and vacuum.
6. Take down decorations and throw away trash.

How to get started:

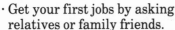

· Get your first jobs by asking relatives or family friends.
· Learn more about party planning, food service, and decorating by reading books and magazines.
· Talk to people who cook or bake for parties, weddings, or special events. Ask questions or offer to go along as a helper, just to learn.

Soon you will be getting calls from people who saw you at parties they attended or from people who heard about you. The best advertising is a good recommendation from a happy customer.

KID BIZ #67: SITTER LIST

Parents of small children are always looking for babysitters. A sitter list is what they need.

Why not make a list and sell it? Parents can save time finding sitters, and sitters can get more jobs.

Here's how to get started:

1. First compile the best and most complete sitter list possible. Include sitters of all ages, young sitters and adult sitters.

2. Include day-care centers, mother's-day-out programs, and city recreational programs that offer "drop in" babysitting services.

3. As you make the list, contact each sitter. Each person who wants to be on the list should pay a small fee. Those who want to include extra advertising should pay a higher rate.

4. Use some of the money the sitters pay in advance to get the lists printed. Protect the lists by putting them in plastic report covers.

5. Now get out there and sell everywhere you go! Put signs on bulletin boards. Wear a T-shirt advertising your business. Talk to your neighbors.

Your sitter list is full of valuable information. Update your list at least two times a year and sell it again!

KID BIZ #68: LEAF RAKING

In the fall, yard mowing gradually comes to an end. But that's not the end of money to be made from yard work. The big opportunity now is in raking leaves.

If the average earnings for leaf removal are $5 to $10 a yard, and most yards need to be raked twice a week, *how much can you earn?*

EARNINGS	1 YD	2 YDS	3 YDS	4 YDS
$5 a yard:	$5	$10	$15	$20
$10 a yard:	$10	$20	$30	$40
$15 a yard:	$15	$30	$45	$60
$20 a yard:	$20	$40	$60	$80

POSSIBLE WEEKLY INCOME

Now figure that the average leaf-raking season lasts six weeks. Multiply each amount on the chart by six. With several regular customers, you could "rake in" $30 to $480 before Christmas!

KID BIZ #69: GARDEN MULCH

Don't throw away those bags of leaves you rake in the fall! Somebody will buy those leaves to mulch their garden for the winter.

(Continued)

Why gardeners buy mulch:

· Covering the garden with a thick layer of mulch helps control weeds, enrich the soil, and hold in water.

· Gardeners are always looking for ways to save on mulching. Ask someone you know with a garden to buy your bags of leaves. You may earn extra money delivering them and spreading them on the garden.

Bonus idea: Gardeners will also buy bags of pine straw, hay, and ground tree bark.

KID BIZ #70: PECANS

Did you ever dream there was really such a thing as a money tree? There *is!*

You can find them — mostly in the fall — in vacant lots, parks, school grounds, near office buildings, along your street, maybe in your back yard.

You won't see dollar bills hanging on these trees, but you will see something just as good: PECANS.

Pecan-selling tips:

· People will buy pecans and other nuts from you in the fall as fast as you can gather them. They want them for their holiday baking.

· Watch for places to get pecans free. Then sell your pecans for a little less than the stores, and you will have plenty of money for Christmas!

KID BIZ #71: STORM CLEANUP

After a storm, there's always lots of yard cleanup to do!

If your area gets severe weather, such as a damaging wind storm, hail storm, or hurricane, you will have lots of chances to earn some money.

Here's how to help:

· Rake and bag leaves and small twigs.
· Gather trash and small limbs.
· Cut up larger limbs and stack wood.

If you've had a bad storm, every yard in your community will need cleanup. In fact, there will be enough work to keep you and ten more kids busy!

KID BIZ #72: BIRD FEEDERS

It's fun to watch birds, and the best way to attract them is with a bird feeder.

Common items you get at the grocery store can be used to create bird feeders to sell.

Try coating a pine cone with peanut butter, then roll in bird seed and add a hanger. Milk cartons make handy feeders also. Books at the library will give you lots of great ideas.

KID BIZ #73: RECIPE BOOKS

 Cooking is an important part of daily living. People are always looking for new ideas, new tastes, and new ways to prepare food. It keeps cooking from being boring.

That's why recipe books are always good sellers. If you enjoy cooking, make and sell your own recipe book!

How to get started:

1. Tell friends, neighbors, and relatives that you are writing a recipe book. Ask each one to contribute one or two favorite recipes.

2. Add cooking hints, measurement tables, pen and ink illustrations, and your own favorite recipes. Copy all recipes carefully and tell the contributor's name.

3. Pages can be hand-lettered, typed, or produced on your computer. The cover should have the title in large letters and a picture or drawing.

4. Have the pages printed at a copy shop. Use colored paper for the cover. Put the books together and staple.

5. Sell your books to people in your neighborhood, your relatives, and even college students with their first apartment. Each person who had recipes published will want to buy books too.

When you go door-to-door to sell books, take a plate of candies or cookies made from a recipe in the book. Offer samples, and people will buy the book just to get that great recipe!

KID BIZ #74: WOOD CRAFTS

Anytime you can take something someone else no longer wants and turn it into cash, you're a *winner*.

Scrap wood is thrown away all the time at construction sites, at businesses, and even in neighborhood trash bins.

If you enjoy wood crafts, this is your opportunity.

Things you can make with wood scraps:

- Bird houses
- Blocks and puzzles
- Toy cars and trains
- Lollipop "trees"
- Pencil holders

- Tie racks
- Doll houses
- Stools
- Picture frames
- Mini-skate ramps

More ideas:

1. Get good wood craft ideas from reading magazines and books. Many give exact plans, drawings, and measurements.

2. Visit craft shows or fairs and notice what are the latest "hot" trends in wood crafting.

3. Since you are getting your wood for free, you can't lose anything by experimenting. Be creative.

4. Sell your wood craft items to neighbors and friends, at craft shows, or door-to-door.

KID BIZ #75: COLLECT ALUMINUM

A lot of people are getting smart about saving those aluminum cans!

But cans aren't the only aluminum items that you can sell to recycling centers. Look for pie plates, frozen food trays, lawn chair frames, pots and pans, rain gutters, house siding, and window screens.

Finding aluminum:

· Leave a special bag or box with neighbors and businesses and ask them to save cans. Go back and collect at the same time each week.

· Find aluminum cans along the road, in ditches, near construction sites, at parks and picnic areas, in parking lots, and trash bins.

· Get permission to have all the cans that are thrown away at large company picnics, parties, or community events.

Selling aluminum:

1. Crush cans to save space. Separate cans from other aluminum items. If you're not sure it's aluminum, test with a magnet. It won't stick.

2. Check with several recycling centers to get the best price for your aluminum. Save until you have a large amount and make one trip.

KID BIZ #76: PAPER AND PLASTIC

Recycling is a habit that puts cash in your pocket, and helps our country use its natural resources more wisely.

Start saving recyclables your family or school usually throws away. It's becoming more and more profitable to turn *trash* into *cash!*

Recycling paper products:

· Newsprint is recyclable, not glossy paper. Keep it dry, and bundle in stacks less than one foot high. Tie with twine or place in paper bags.
· Cardboard should be flattened, bundled, and tied with twine.
· Office paper and computer paper is also recyclable, but should be bundled separately from other kinds of paper.
· Although the price you get for paper is low, it is a heavy product and mounts up fast.

Recycling plastic products:

· The plastic recycling industry is now in the beginning stages. It will soon become as common to recycle plastic as it is paper.

· Plastic bottles, milk jugs, and cafeteria trays are now being shredded and used in carpeting, furniture stuffing, insulated clothing, home insulation, and making "plastic lumber" for outdoor furniture and decks.

KID BIZ #77: DELIVERING FLYERS

Did you ever wonder how all those business flyers and cards get on your front door?

Well, someone gets *paid* to put them there!

And that should give you an idea, because you could do a job like that. Businesses and people running for political office often hire young people — just like you — to deliver special messages to the front doors in your neighborhood.

GRAND OPENING SALE!

Steps to success:

1. Ask people who own a business or participate in local politics. Tell them you want to work.

2. Or contact businesses that leave flyers on your door — and ask.

3. Always work with a partner. You take one side of the street, and your partner takes the other. The job goes faster that way.

4. Stay on the exact streets you are assigned. Never leave the area or go inside any home or business.

5. If you want to be offered the job again, work steady and be enthusiastic.

✳ FOR MORE INFORMATION ✳

American Institute of Small Business, 7515 Wayzata Blvd., Suite 201, Minneapolis, MN 55426. Ask for information on materials that tell kids how to set up their own business.

Business Kids, P.O. Box 149003, Coral Gables, FL 33114. Ask for information on "The Business Kit."

Center for Business and Economic Education, Lubbock Christian College, 5601 W. 19th St., Lubbock, TX 79407. Kids may request information on "How to Grow a Business." Teachers may request information on "The Chocolate Factory" kit for classroom use.

Consumer Information Center, P.O. Box 100, Pueblo, CO 81002. Ask for free consumer information catalog.

Entrepreneur Magazine, P.O. Box 50368, Boulder, CO 80321-0368. News about entrepreneurs of all ages.

Freebies Magazine, P.O. Box 20283, Santa Barbara, CA 93120. Lists free or low cost sources for craft materials and kits.

Inventors Workshop, 3201 Corte Malpaso, Suite 304, Camarillo, CA 93010. Send a self-addressed stamped envelope. Ask for information for young inventors.

National Center for Financial Education, P.O. Box KB-34070, San Diego, CA 92103. Send a self-addressed stamped envelope. Ask for a free issue of the newsletter, "Motivator."

Small Business Development Center. Call toll-free 1-800-368-5855. Give your area code and get the phone number of your local office. Provides free counseling to any businessperson.

✱ FOR FURTHER READING ✱

A Real Job For You by Rose P. Lee. An employment guide to help teens find their first "real" job. Betterway Pub., P.O. Box 219, Crozet, VA 22932.

Birthday Parties by Vicki Lansky. Decorations, themes, games, and food for kids' parties. Practical Parenting, Dept. 5M-89, 18326 Minnetonka Blvd., Deephaven, MN 55391.

Designer Sweatshirts by Mary Mulari. Learn basic applique and turn sweatshirts into special garments that are fun to make and wear. Mary Productions, Box 87, 217 No. Main, Aurora, MN 55705.

From Rags to Riches: People Who Started Businesses From Scratch, the Inside Business Series. Stories of ordinary people who started businesses and became wealthy. Lerner Publications, 241 First Ave. No., Minneapolis, MN 55401.

Inventors Guidebook by Mel Fuller. Step-by-step explanation of the inventing process. M & M Assc., 9707 Quartz Valley Rd., Ft. Jones, CA 96032.

Making Birdhouses and Feeders by Charles R. Self. Easy designs and instructions for forty-one different kinds of birdhouses and feeders. Sterling Publishing Co., 387 Park Ave. South, New York, NY 10016.

Smart Spending by Lois Schmitt. Guide to consumer issues for ages ten to fourteen. Atheneum Books, Macmillan Publishing Co., 866 Third Ave., New York, NY 10022.

The Teenage Entrepreneur's Guide by Sarah Riehm. Fifty business plans for older teens who want to start their own business. Surrey Books, 101 E. Erie, Suite 900, Chicago, IL 60611.

DOOR-TO-DOOR
SAFETY

1. Always tell an adult exactly where you will be and when you will return.

2. Be dependable about staying in the area where you said you would be.

3. If you are working in a new area, team up with a friend.

4. Talk to customers at the front door.

5. Never go inside or accept food or drinks.

6. If you think you will need to take a break, plan to stop at a well-traveled local business.

7. Never get in a car with anyone without permission from your parents.

8. Carry change for a phone call.

9. If you feel strange or uneasy about *any* situation, leave immediately.

10. Keep money hidden in a safe place. Leave extra money at home.

11. Always be alert to what is happening around you.

12. Plan for *safety first!*

CHAPTER 7

WINTER MONEY-MAKING PROJECTS

What's good about winter money-making projects? Cold weather doesn't stop people from spending money or needing extra help. In fact, the winter holidays make this a fun and profitable time to be a young entrepreneur.

Tips on Winter Money-making Opportunities

· *It's time to shop.* People will buy almost any gift item. Sell tree decorations, mistletoe, pine cones, or gift certificates. Make custom greeting cards or stationery.

· *It's time for a snow removal service.* A list of regular customers who need your help every time it snows will keep you in the money. For bonus income, sell firewood.

· *It's time for indoor projects.* Be a study buddy, an exercise partner, a mother's helper, or a maid-for-a-day.

· *Winter holidays* are Christmas, New Year's Day, and Valentine's Day. Try gift wrapping, taking photos at parties, assembling bikes and trikes, or holiday house cleaning.

DECEMBER

GOAL #1: _____

SUNDAY	MONDAY	TUESDAY	WEDNESDAY

GOAL #2: _____

NOTES

THURSDAY	FRIDAY	SATURDAY

JANUARY

GOAL #1: _____

SUNDAY	MONDAY	TUESDAY	WEDNESDAY

GOAL #2: _____			NOTES
THURSDAY	FRIDAY	SATURDAY	

FEBRUARY

GOAL #1: _____

SUNDAY	MONDAY	TUESDAY	WEDNESDAY

GOAL #2: _____			NOTES
THURSDAY	FRIDAY	SATURDAY	

TO-DO LIST

KID BIZ #78: GIFT CERTIFICATES

The winter holiday season is a great time to sell gift certificates. You get paid *before* you do the work!

GIFT CERTIFICATE

This certificate is worth ONE FREE EVENING *of babysitting.* CALL Ann: 422-2343

How to get started:

1. Decide what kind of gift certificates to sell. They can be worth a free car wash, free house cleaning, free babysitting — any job you want.

2. Use the design on this page or design your own gift certificate. Decide how much to charge.

3. Sell door-to-door or to friends and relatives. Ask people you have worked for too. This time of year, people will buy them for gifts.

4. Sell more by offering a bargain price for buying more than one certificate. For example, if your price is $6 each, sell two for $10. Or make books of certificates.

5. The person who receives the gift certificate will call you about the job. Be sure to sell only the number of gift certificates you can fulfill!

6. Schedule a time and do the job you have promised quickly and cheerfully.

KID BIZ #79: CARDS AND STATIONERY

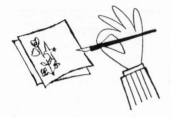

Do you like to draw, make designs, or sketch cartoons? Use your favorites to create cards and stationery items.

Handmade greeting cards sell well, especially during the Christmas season.

Steps to success:

1. You don't have to be an expert artist. People like simple designs on greeting cards, note cards, and stationery.

2. Buy blank cards and stationery papers at an art supply or office supply store. Smooth finished papers are best. For variety later on, try colored papers.

3. Try your designs on scratch paper. For stationery, note paper, and thank you cards, a simple design in one corner or a border is enough. For greeting cards, use larger drawings.

4. Try folding the cards and paper different ways. When you have finished planning the designs, you can start drawing on the good paper.

5. Sell the stationery in sets. Offer the cards separate or in packages of eight to ten.

6. Sell door-to-door or at craft shows and fairs. Tell people you also take custom orders.

KID BIZ #80: GIFT WRAPPING

Your friends, neighbors, and family members will like this idea. You can save them time and money on gift wrapping during the busy Christmas season.

How to get started:

1. Get ideas for attractive gift wraps by visiting gift wrap counters and browsing through holiday magazines.

2. Buy paper, ribbon, and bows on sale. Start saving boxes of all sizes and shapes.

3. Make a price list showing what you charge for different sizes, special jobs, or hard-to-wrap items. (Gift bags may be the answer.)

4. Some people may supply the wrap and pay you by the hour. Your prices should be low enough to be a bargain, but high enough to make it worth the work.

5. Let people know about your service with flyers and notes on bulletin boards.

6. Have several empty boxes wrapped as samples, so customers can choose what they like.

7. Remember people are counting on you to have their packages ready on time, so keep up with the work every day.

Bonus idea: A store or small shop in your area may allow you to have a gift wrap table on a Saturday during the Christmas shopping season. They will provide the supplies and pay you to do the work.

KID BIZ #81: TREE DECORATIONS

START EARLY

No matter how many tree decorations people have, they always like to buy more.

If you like crafts, you'll have fun making decorations to sell at Christmas, but start early!

Steps to success:

1. Get ideas from Christmas craft books and magazines. Visit craft stores and craft shows to see what kinds of decorations are popular.

2. As you consider what to make, think about your skills, how much the materials cost, and how long it takes to make each item.

3. People are always looking for unusual handmade decorations, especially if you can personalize the item with the customer's name and the date.

4. Make up samples of several decorations and show them to friends and neighbors the first week of December. Start taking orders.

5. Try to fill orders quickly, so people can finish decorating their homes well before Christmas. Your decorations will also make good gifts for teachers, co-workers, and neighbors.

Suggested ornaments: Mini-wreaths, clothes-pin reindeers, crocheted Santas, painted wood stars or stockings, fancy bows, angels, ceramic figures, or stuffed fabric gingerbread men. You might also offer garlands for the tree.

KID BIZ #82: MISTLETOE

In the winter when the trees are bare, you will see "green clumps" way up in some trees. That's *mistletoe.*

People love to buy mistletoe at Christmas. It gives them an excuse to *kiss!*

Steps to success:

1. Mistletoe sells best one week before Christmas, and especially on Christmas Eve Day.

2. Keep it fresh by gathering only what you can sell each day. If you have to keep it overnight, put it in a plastic bag in the refrigerator.

3. Sell mistletoe by the sprig or in small bags for $.50 to $1. Offer larger bunches for $2 and up.

4. Tie red bows on the sprigs or decorate with colorful Christmas streamers, and your mistletoe will bring even better prices.

5. Sell your mistletoe in front of the busiest store in your neighborhood, or go door-to-door.

6. Show a cheerful holiday spirit when you go out to sell. People will appreciate your attitude and feel more generous.

Bonus idea: If you know where there is a holly tree, you can sell holly too. Starting the second week in December, sell large bunches for $3 and up.

Note: Make certain that you have approval to "harvest" the trees bearing mistletoe.

KID BIZ #83: CARRY BAGS AND PACKAGES

Watch for people who need help carrying bags and packages during the busy Christmas shopping season.

This is a project you can do anywhere, but busy shopping centers will bring you the most customers.

Steps to success:

1. People most likely to need your help are mothers with small children, senior citizens, someone on crutches, or people going upstairs.
2. Let the customer decide how much to pay. Most people will be very generous.
3. Help some people even if they can't pay. You will be rewarded in other ways.
4. Handle bags and packages carefully. Always say thanks when you are paid.

KID BIZ #84: BIKE ASSEMBLY

Have you thought about who is going to put Susie's new trike together this Christmas? If you know how to work on bikes, you can earn some Christmas cash assembling bikes and trikes for busy parents.

- Get started by asking friends and neighbors.
- Read instructions before you begin. Only accept jobs that you understand how to do.
- Remember people are counting on you to finish in time for Christmas. Be dependable.

KID BIZ #85: PINE CONES

Pine cones are popular items for decorating or using to make wreaths for Christmas. And people like to set baskets full of them by the fireplace during the winter.

They're *free*. So just go pick some up and start selling!

Steps to success:
1. Collect pine cones of different sizes. Spray paint some of your pine cones white, gold, or red. And leave some natural.
2. If you have old candles, melt them down and dip pine cones in the wax. People buy these to use in their fireplaces. It makes the fire beautiful.
3. Sell to craft stores, in front of busy stores on weekends, or door-to-door.
4. For bonus income, sell sweet gum balls too.

KID BIZ #86: PHOTOS

Have a camera? *Take pictures!* People love pictures of their kids, their pets, and themselves.

Take photos at Christmas programs, parties, reunions, and dinners. If your camera develops film instantly, sell pictures on the spot. If not, get people's name and address and go back later to sell the photos.

KID BIZ #87: CANDLE CRAFTS

This project could be called a *bright* idea, for sure, because making and selling your own candle creations is fun! People like to buy candles for gifts or to decorate their homes. Unusual or unique candles are often collected as a hobby. Your candle creations will be in great demand at Christmas.

How to make candles:

1. Collect old candles or buy wax by the block. Bend the rim of an empty coffee can to form a spout. Put wax in the coffee can. Place on a rack in a pot of water. Melt wax over low heat.

2. Tint the wax with old crayons. Or you can buy dyes and scents from a craft store.

3. Use a 1/2-gal. or 1-qt. milk carton for a mold. Prepare the wick by tying a heavy washer or fishing weight to one end. Suspend it over the center of your mold with a pencil.

4. For an interesting and unusual candle, fill the mold with ice cubes. Then carefully pour hot wax into the mold without disturbing the wick.

5. Allow candles to cool overnight. Tear the paper carton away from the candle and drain water.

6. Decorate with ribbon, Christmas greenery, silk flowers, glitter, or whipped wax. Sell to friends and neighbors or take special orders.

KID BIZ #88: SNOW REMOVAL

In the winter the most profitable outdoor work for young people is snow removal. With a list of regular customers, you can earn good money in bad weather!

To get started you need warm clothes, a good snow shovel, and an ice scraper. Then team up with a hard-working friend and see how much you can earn.

How to get customers:

1. Make some flyers announcing your snow removal service and pass them out in your neighborhood. Then go back to sign up regular customers who will agree to let you do all their snow removal.
2. For extra jobs, visit small businesses in your area early in the morning after a snow and see if they need help.

Doing the job:

· Get more done by working with a partner, especially on heavy snow days.
· Your job should include chopping off ice on dangerous steps. The customer may also have salt you can sprinkle on steps or walk areas.
· Snow shoveling is heavy work, so rest when you get tired. Don't take jobs that are gigantic.

Bonus ideas: If your customer is happy with your work, ask him to recommend you to a friend. Don't forget your snow removal customers after winter is over. Contact them when you are helping with gardens in the spring or mowing yards in the summer.

KID BIZ #89: BABYSITTER FINDER

Here's a way to make money on a babysitting business — without doing the sitting! You help parents with babysitter *finding*.

Finding a sitter is often a problem for parents. They will be glad to pay you a small fee for finding them a sitter. And with this plan, it will only take a few phone calls for you to find just the right person for the job.

How to get started:

1. Find out who babysits or wants to babysit in your neighborhood.
2. Talk to each sitter about your list and how it will help them get more jobs.
3. For each person who wants to be on your list, make a card showing their name, address, phone, age, experience, and times available to sit.
4. Advertise your finder service with cards and flyers throughout your neighborhood.

Tips for success:

· Set a price list of basic fees, including a slightly higher fee for rush requests.
· Always start calling for a sitter as soon as you get a request. Your fast service will impress parents to call again.
· Increase profits by charging sitters a small fee each time you get them a job.
· Be looking for new sitters to add to your list all the time.

KID BIZ #90: FIREWOOD

City folks with fireplaces often have to pay high prices for their firewood. You can get firewood free and sell it in your neighborhood.

How to get free firewood:

- Where land is being cleared
- Abandoned trees in the woods
- When a storm blows down trees or large limbs
- A neighbor who has a tree cut down or heavily pruned (get permission)

Selling firewood:

1. Firewood is priced by cubic feet, which means a stack of wood twelve inches high, twelve inches long, and twelve inches wide.

2. Hardwoods sell for higher prices than softer woods. Soft woods are pine and firs. Oak or elm are harder. Fruit tree woods are the hardest.

3. Sell only what you can deliver with a wagon. Or find an adult who can help with transportation as a partner.

4. Make flyers to announce your service and put them out all around your community. Go door-to-door and offer to supply firewood once a week throughout the winter (if you have an adequate supply).

Bonus idea: People will also buy kindling by the bundle or box. Gather small twigs, wood scraps, and branches from wooded areas or lumber yards. Kindling is easy to carry and sell door-to-door.

KID BIZ #91: JANITOR SERVICE

Start a "junior janitor" service for small shops and offices in your community. The pay is good, and you can do several jobs a week.

Doing the job:

1. Work with the business owner to make a checklist of your duties. Then use the checklist as a reminder list every time you work.
2. Things on the checklist might be vacuuming, cleaning windows or display cases, dusting, emptying trash, or cleaning floor mats.

The owners of small businesses do their own cleaning most of the time. At busy times of the year they need help. Some will want you on a regular schedule. Others will need you on a "call-in" basis.

KID BIZ #92: HOUSE CLEANING

House cleaning is one of those unending jobs that's here to stay. More and more busy people are paying someone to clean.

YOU MESS IT UP— WE CLEAN IT UP!

You can cash in on the house cleaning business too. If you have helped with chores at home, you're already trained for the job. It's a sure bet one of your neighbors needs help now!

(Continued)

156

House cleaning success ideas:

· If you want lots of work, pass out flyers in your neighborhood.
· List suggested jobs you can do and your suggested prices. Typical jobs are sweeping, mopping, dusting, washing dishes, cleaning bathrooms, and doing laundry.
· Before you start a job, be sure you know exactly what the customer expects you to do.

Give people a good job and they will tell others about your cleaning service. The busy Christmas holiday season is a good time to build your business.

KID BIZ #93: FURNITURE POLISHING

Some busy people manage to get regular cleaning chores done, but they have to hire help for the extras. One of those extras you can do is polishing furniture or woodwork.

Getting started:

· Use a good furniture polish to practice at home. Then look for customers.
· Put out flyers to announce your special service.
· Ask friends and relatives.
· Check with small businesses.

Gim' me A Break!

Agree on your duties and your prices before you begin. Work steady and be proud of a good job!

KID BIZ #94: BOTTLES AND JARS

Don't throw anything away! Recycle it!

Glass bottles and jars can be recycled too. These "throw-aways" can be sold for *cash* — just what you need!

Ways to recycle bottles and jars:

· Many jars are just the right size for canning.
· Bottles can be used to make candle holders, vases, or lamps.
· Some bottles are valuable for collecting or for decorating antique shops or restaurants.
· Recycling centers buy glass by the pound. Collect clear, amber, and green bottles and jars. Rinse and keep in separate boxes.

KID BIZ #95: CAN LABELS AND BOX TOPS

Refunders love trash! They save can labels and box tops from food and household products. Then they get cash refunds, free groceries, and cents-off coupons from companies that offer refunds all over the U.S.

Study the refund offers on the bulletin board at the grocery store. Start saving the packaging from products you use. Then sell your trash to refunders in your community. Find them by placing a notice on the bulletin board near the refund offers.

KID BIZ #96: STUDY BUDDY

If you are a good student, you can earn money helping other kids in the subjects that are easy for you!

When students need help, teachers often advise parents to hire a coach or tutor. Advertise yourself as a "study buddy" for kids having trouble in school.

Getting jobs:

- Concentrate on working with kids just a few years younger than you. They will like the idea of a study partner rather than a "tutor."
- Tell teachers about your service and what subjects you coach. They will tell parents.
- You may also find jobs by putting notices on bulletin boards in the community.

Working with students:

1. Agree on a schedule for working together each week. Twice a week for one hour each works well.
2. Agree with the parents on your pay. Adult tutors normally earn $12 to $15 an hour.
3. Stick to your study schedule. Start on time and end on time. A clock nearby will remind you.
4. Parents should be able to tell you where the student needs help and where to start.
5. Teachers will also give suggestions.
6. Try to find ways to make studying fun. Offer small rewards. Make games. Use funny reminders. Praise any improvement.

Consider other coaching jobs if you have skills in music, cheerleading, art, computer, or sports.

159

KID BIZ #97: EXERCISE PARTNER

January is the month when people get real serious about diet and exercise. They join health clubs and hire personal "trainers" to help them get fit.

If you are "into" aerobics, jogging, biking, tennis, or other fitness programs, this is your opportunity.

People who are having trouble keeping their New Year's resolution to get in shape will want your help.

How to get jobs:

1. Make an eye-catching flyer to announce your services as an exercise partner. List types of exercise and your fee per hour.
2. Give out the flyers in your neighborhood.
3. Ask local beauty shops or barber shops if you can leave flyers on the counter.
4. Call senior citizens' groups and offer to attend a meeting and demonstrate your exercises.
5. Ask neighbors or relatives who are dieting.

Doing the job:

· People hire you to help them stay on their routine. Make a schedule and be faithful about arriving on time and being ready to work.
· People hire you because they don't like to exercise alone. Be energetic and cheerful. They will look forward to the exercise sessions.
· People hire you because they don't know how to do the new exercises. Teach them how.

KID BIZ #98: MOTHER'S HELPER

How about a job where you get paid to play?

That's what being a mother's helper is all about! Your job is to entertain the child in another part of the house so the busy mother can have some time to herself.

Steps to success:

1. Give out flyers saying you like kids and want to be a mother's helper. Make your flyers colorful and unique, so people will remember you better.
2. Plan some games, stories, and quiet activities for little children.
3. Some mother's helpers take along a "surprise bag" with interesting things you find around the house: modeling clay, a funny hat, earrings or ribbons to play dress up, a puppet, or art supplies and colored paper.
4. Ask the mother for special instructions. Then try not to interrupt her at all.
5. Learn all you can about children by watching the mother and asking questions.
6. Take a babysitting course this winter through your local Red Cross, hospital, or YMCA.

Being a mother's helper is one of the best ways to get experience at babysitting. And the mother is always there if you need her!

KID BIZ #99: VALENTINE CRAFTS

Valentine's Day is another holiday people love to celebrate with gifts. If you want to make and sell craft items for Valentine's Day, get geared up in early January.

Suggested craft ideas:

- Anything heart-shaped will sell: refrigerator magnets, tiny sachet pillows, jewelry, or party decorations.
- People will also buy almost any item decorated with hearts: pencils, stuffed animals, sweat shirts, baskets, or photo album covers.
- Save money on craft materials by using things you have at home: bits of lace, scraps of red material, felt, glitter, and sequins.

How to get started:

1. Look through magazines and craft books for Valentine's ideas. Get other ideas by visiting craft stores, gift shops, and art supply shops.
2. Try to find one or two small craft items that are fast, easy, and low in cost.
3. Make samples of the items you are considering to see if the idea really works.
4. If you are pleased with the results, start showing your samples to friends and neighbors.
5. Decide on prices for your Valentine crafts and start taking orders.
6. Try to fill orders immediately. Your customers will pass the word about your business, and the results will be more sales.

KID BIZ #100: VALENTINE MESSAGES

You can make a lot of people happy on Valentine's Day by delivering Valentine messages and gifts!

Start planning in late January and take orders February 1–12.

Steps to success:

1. Announce your service with flyers and cards. High school and college students are some of your most likely customers.

2. Make a list of suggested deliveries and your fees. Some ideas are Valentine candy, cards, flowers, stuffed animals, or other gifts.

3. Decide whether you will also supply the flowers or gifts. You can often arrange a special deal with a florist if you buy in large quantities.

4. Take orders during the two weeks before Valentine's Day. Schedule the deliveries and make notes on special instructions.

5. Two days before Valentine's Day, pick up all items to be delivered and tag them with names and addresses.

6. Plan something special to wear for deliveries.

7. When you make a delivery, have people sign for the article.

If you have fun, are creative, and use imagination, your Valentine message service will make big money!

KID BIZ #101: MAID-FOR-A-DAY

Everyone thinks it would be fun to have a maid. So start a service called Maid-for-a-Day. Then people will hire you to be their personal assistant for the day.

Suggested work: Housework, laundry, ironing, shopping, cooking, kitchen cleanup, errands, closet cleaning, babysitting, giving a manicure, clipping coupons, bathing the dog, watering the plants, baking a cake, shining shoes, or helping with a party.

How to get started:

1. Give out business cards and flyers describing your service and your fee for a day. Relatives and neighbors will be good first customers.

2. This will be a weekend job only, unless you offer additional hourly rates. Then people could hire you for a few hours after school.

3. You might also offer this service on a gift certificate. Maid-for-a-Day would make a wonderful birthday or anniversary present!

Bonus idea: When your Maid-for-a-Day starts growing, hire other people to be the maids. Then you can spend your time getting more business!

✓✓ BABYSITTING REMINDERS

1. Get to know the family before you accept the job.

2. Make an agreement on time, pay, and special responsibilities.

3. Get safety and emergency instructions before parents leave.

4. Use play to distract an unhappy child.

5. Take phone messages for parents, but don't tell a caller you are alone.

6. Never open the door for anyone.

7. Stay awake. Check on sleeping children at least every half hour.

8. Don't stay on the phone. Parents may need to call.

9. Give medicine only if instructed by parents.

10. Never leave a baby alone on a dressing table, bed, or chair.

11. Phone for help or advice any time you are in doubt about a situation.

12. Plan to have reliable transportation home when the parents return.

✳ FOR MORE INFORMATION ✳

Center for Innovation and Business Development, Box 8103, University Station, Grand Forks, ND 58202. Ask for information on the "Entrepreneur Kit."

Christmas Newsletters, Bold Productions, P.O. Box 152281, Arlington, TX 76015. Send a self-addressed stamped envelope. Ask for Christmas newsletters about gifts, wraps, and decorations.

Extra Income Magazine, P.O. Box 3746, Escondido, CA 92025. Read about young people and adults who have started part-time businesses.

Federal Reserve Bank of New York, Public Information Dept., 33 Liberty St., New York, NY 10045. Send a postcard. Request "Coins & Currency" booklet.

Kid Biz Software, Homeland Publications, 1808 Capri Ln., Seabrook, TX 77586. Send a self-addressed stamped envelope. Ask for information on computer software for *Kid Biz.* Choose a business idea, print business cards, keep track of customers and appointments, and manage your money business.

Money Management Institute, Household International, 2700 Sanders Rd., Prospect Heights, IL 60070. Ask for information on booklet, "Children and Money Management."

New Business Opportunities Magazine, P.O. Box 50347, Boulder, CO 80321-0347. Articles on starting a new business and new business ideas.

Service Corps of Retired Executives (Score). Call toll-free 1-800-368-5855. Give your area code and get the phone number of your local office. Provides free counseling for anyone interested in business.

FOR FURTHER READING

Capitalism For Kids by Karl Hess. Explains the free-enterprise system and the benefits of "hands-on" learning about business at an early age. Enterprise Publishing, 725 Market Street, Wilmington, DE 19801.

Dear Babysitter by Vicki Lansky. Babysitter's handbook that explains babysitting techniques, first-aid information, and has a fifty-page instruction pad. Meadowbrook Press, 18318 Minnetonka Blvd., Deephaven, MN 55391.

Great Gift Wrapping by Burglind Neirmann. Fully illustrated instructions on basics of gift wrapping and unusual wraps. Sterling Publishing Co., 387 Park Ave. South, New York, NY 10016.

Guide to Self-Employment by Robert L. Perry. Interesting stories of young people who have started businesses. Complete how-to's on starting a business. Franklin Watts, 387 Park Ave. South, New York, NY 10016.

Is There Life After Housework? by Don Aslett. Step-by-step instructions for cleaning every area of the home. Writer's Digest Books, 1507 Dana Ave., Cincinnati, OH 45207.

Making Cents: Every Kid's Guide to Money by Elizabeth Wilkinson. Facts about money and spare time money-making ideas. Little, Brown & Co., 200 West St., Waltham, MA 02254.

The Kid's Money Book by Neale S. Godfrey. Everything from the history of money to investing in the stock market. Checkerboard Press, Macmillan Publishing Co., 866 Third Ave., New York, NY 10022.

Need Help?
CALL - A - KID !

QUESTIONS AND ANSWERS

1. What if I don't have enough money to start a business?

Most of the businesses described in our book don't need much money to start. Some don't require any. If you have chosen an idea that takes money to start, here are some ways to find cash:

- Turn things you don't use anymore into cash by having a giant garage sale.
- Ask your parents or neighbors if they have any extra jobs you can do for some quick cash.
- Save your allowance and birthday money.
- Negotiate a small loan from your parents. Write up a contract showing how and when you will repay the money.

2. What "legal stuff" do I need to check on before I start a business?

If you plan to operate your business under a name other than your own, you need to go to the office of the County Clerk and file a special form called a "doing business as" or DBA form.

For information on taxes, licenses, or permits that may be required, call your local Chamber of Commerce. Any self-employed person who earns over $400 a year must report the income and pay income tax.

3. Should I open a bank account?

Most young people do not need a checking account to run a business. A savings account, however, is an excellent place to keep the money you earn.

4. Can I use my home computer in my business?

A computer will help you run almost every part of your business. You can make business plans, customer lists, calendars and schedules, print receipts, keep records, and make flyers. The only thing it won't do is go out and push the lawnmower!

A special computer software package has been designed to go with this book. Ask for KID'S BUSINESS software at your bookstore. Or contact the publisher (Disk-Count Software, 1751 W. County Rd. B, Suite 107, St. Paul, MN 55113/1-800-333-8776).

5. How much time should I spend on my business?

During the school year, ten to fifteen hours a week is enough. The child labor laws protect children from being hired by employers or working long hours at an early age. For information on how the child labor laws affect your business, contact your local Department of Labor office.

6. Which KID BIZ projects are good for beginners?

Beginners should try simple helping projects such as numbers 29, 33, 34, 68, 83, and 98. Selling things is another good way to get started (numbers 13, 15, 22, 26, 48, 57, 70, 82, and 85). The recycling projects listed on page 173 are also good for beginners.

7. Which KID BIZ projects are for young entrepreneurs who want a challenge?

If you want a challenge try KID BIZ numbers 8, 11, 19, 25, 41, 45, 46, 56, 66, 84, 86, 97, or 100. Also, the BONUS IDEAS at the end of many projects offer good suggestions for expanding your business.

8. What organizations help young people learn to manage money or start a business?

Girl Scouts and Boy Scouts work toward badges that teach money and business. Junior Achievement programs ("Business Basics" and "Project Business") are excellent for kids who are interested in business. And the 4-H program has "Learn to Earn" units of study. If you are interested in business as a career, consider taking as many business courses as possible in high school.

9. What is the most common job done by young people?

Research says almost half the kids who work part-time start out with lawn mowing or yard work. Most kids learn how to do these jobs at home. Then it's easy to go out and get jobs in the neighborhood.

10. What's the secret to having happy customers?

- Be cheerful and courteous. Show that you are interested in doing a good job.
- Discuss the job and the pay before you start.
- Be dependable to do your jobs on time.
- Follow special instructions carefully.
- Be careful not to damage property.
- Clean up after your job.
- Always say thanks and set an appointment for the next time.

11. What kind of money-making opportunities should I look for in my neighborhood?

Look for things people are too busy to do and things people don't like to do. They'll hire you to do it for them!

12. Why is cleaning such a booming business today?

Everything gets dirty! Cleaning is easy to learn. (Practice at home. Your parents will love it.) Cleaning is in great demand as more people are working longer hours outside the home. (More people are also paying someone to clean up their mess.) It's an unlimited money-making prospect. (Everything gets dirty over and over again!)

13. Does this book give any ideas for posters or flyers to advertise my business?

Yes, as you look through the 101 *Kid Biz* projects you will see many ideas for eye-catching designs. You can also get good ideas by looking through the yellow pages of your phone book, from magazine ads, and from reading the newspaper. When you get a good idea, draw a quick sketch and keep it for future use.

14. Where can I write to get answers to other questions about starting a business?

The authors of this book publish a newsletter called *Kids Mean Business*. Write them a letter asking your hardest money questions or telling your best money ideas. Enclose a self-addressed stamped envelope and they will send you a free newsletter. The address is KIDS MEAN BUSINESS, Dept. E-KB, 1808 Capri Ln., Seabrook, TX 77586.

15. What does it really mean to be a "success?"

To some young people, success is having money and things. But there's much more to success than things. It means reaching a goal, making your plan work, doing your best. It means you're a winner, because you take charge of your life and try your very best.

WHAT I LIKE TO DO

I LIKE:	KID BIZ NUMBERS:
Animals	7, 14, 34, 35, 50, 51, 64, 86
Cleaning things	2, 3, 5, 30, 41, 42, 46, 52, 66, 71, 91, 92, 93, 101
Cooking	26, 57, 58, 65, 73, 101
Entertaining	11, 17, 26, 45, 56, 66, 100
Fixing things	24, 25, 43, 61, 62, 71, 72, 84
Helping people	1, 6, 8, 9, 10, 11, 17, 19, 28, 29, 32, 33, 43, 61, 63, 65, 66, 67, 83, 89, 91, 96, 97, 98, 101
Making things	18, 31, 45, 53, 55, 60, 72, 73, 74, 79, 80, 81, 87, 99
Outdoor jobs	4, 8, 10, 22, 27, 40, 41, 42, 43, 50, 51, 52, 64, 70, 77, 90
Recycling	5, 16, 23, 25, 47, 48, 49, 75, 76, 90, 94, 95
School	19, 45, 53, 54, 59, 79, 96
Selling things	7, 15, 16, 18, 20, 21, 26, 31, 45, 47, 48, 53, 54, 57, 58, 59, 60, 67, 70, 78, 82, 85, 86, 99
Sports	8, 9, 10, 15, 53, 64, 97
Working together	1, 2, 3, 16, 20, 27, 28, 30, 41, 47, 48, 52, 56, 62, 77, 90
Yard work	6, 12, 13, 20, 21, 36, 37, 38, 39, 44, 68, 69, 71, 88

MONEY DIARY

DATE	AMOUNT	PURCHASE	IN BUDGET?

MONEY WORDS

Action steps: Plans and activities for the purpose of reaching a definite result or goal.

Advertise: To announce publicly; to tell about, usually with cards, signs, flyers, and ads.

Agreement: A fixing of terms on a business deal so that everyone understands.

Announcement: A proclaiming or telling about something so that everyone knows.

Attention-getters: Advertising that grabs attention because it is unusual or inventive.

Balancing the budget: Making sure the amount to be spent does not add up to more than the income.

Banner: A large sign with one line of advertising in very large letters.

Bargain: Something offered or gotten for much less than the usual price.

Bazaar: A special sale put on by a nonprofit organization to raise money by selling food, crafts, and handmade gift items.

Benefits: Ways a product or service will help a customer or improve the quality of life.

Bonus: Something extra; beyond what was expected.

Brochure: A small booklet or one sheet of advertising material folded to look like a booklet.

Budget: A careful plan for spending money that you earn or receive.

Business: Activities of selling a product or service in order to make a profit.

Business plan: A written description of a business idea and what it will take to organize and run the business profitably.

Career: Life's work; profession; the way one earns a living.

Call-in basis: An agreement to be available to work for someone when they need you and call.

Combination: A grouping of related jobs or businesses.

Community: All of the people who live in a particular area of a town.

Consumer: A person who buys goods for his own needs.

Corporation: A business owned by a group of people called stockholders.

Co-workers: Persons who work or labor together.

Create: To make, form, put together.

Custom order: Specially made for people according to their requests.

Customer: A person who buys a product or service from a business.

Deadline: The latest time that something is to be done.

Decisions: Choices made after considering the facts.

Demonstration: Showing how something works; showing how a job is done and explaining the steps.

Dependable: Trusted; to be relied on.

Design: An arrangement of colors and drawings; a decoration or pattern.

Donate: To give to some good cause or charity.

Door-to-door: Going from home to home to sell a product or tell people about a service.

Employer: Person or company you work for.

Entrepreneur: A person who organizes and manages a business undertaking; an inventor of a business.

Estimate: To make a general but careful guess about the price of a job or the cost of supplies.

Expand: To enlarge; to grow bigger.

Expense: Money spent or needed for carrying out a job or running a business.

Fad: A style that many people are interested in for a short time.

Fair wage: Being paid according to what is right or normal for a certain job.

Fee: A charge for some service.

Fill-in: To take someone's place and do their job while they are gone.

Flea market: A street market for cheap or second-hand items.

Flyer: A sheet of paper printed with advertising for a business.

Formula: A rule; set of directions.

Freebie: Something a business gives out free to get customers' attention, usually something small and inexpensive.

Garage sale: A home sale of used items at bargain prices.

Gift certificate: A written or printed statement that can be traded for service or products — usually bought to be given to someone.

Gift items: Small things people will buy to give as presents.

Goal: A target to aim for; a desired result; a purpose or dream.

Going rate: The amount of money most others are paid for a certain job.

Guaranteed: Promise to be of quality; promising that something will happen.

Hire: To agree to pay money in return for work.

Hobby: Activities done in spare time for fun.

Hourly wage: How much you earn per hour.

Income: The money you get as wages; the profit you make in a business.

Interest: Money paid for the use of money; what the bank pays you for keeping money in a savings account.

Invent: To think up or make something new.

Invest: To spend money or time in order to profit.

Long-term: For an extended period of time.

Manage: To have charge of; control; guide.

Marketing: Everything you do to tell about your business and get customers to buy.

Money diary: A complete list of every amount of money you spend for a period of time; includes date, amount, and items purchased.

Networking: Friends helping friends with business contacts.

Newsletter: A small paper telling information about a certain group of people.

Operate: To keep in action; run; work.

Opportunity: A time or occasion that is right for doing something; a good chance for success.

Orders: A list of requests for products people want to receive.

Organize: Work out the details; make a system.

Organization: A group of persons united and working for a purpose.

Paid advertising: Paying to place an ad in a newspaper or any printed publication.

Pamphlet: A thin booklet with a paper cover.

Partner: A person who shares the work and the pay.

Part-time job: Being employed for only part of the usual work week.

Photocopying: Reproducing printed materials on a machine that takes pictures and gives an instant copy.

Plan: A list of actions or steps you intend to take in order to reach a goal.

Pocket money: Extra money you carry to use for unexpected expenses.

Price list: A set list of the amounts you are asking to be paid.

Priorities: The most important things you need to do.

Product: Something you buy, find, or make that can be sold for profit.

Professional: Someone who earns a living doing a job that requires special education or training.

Profit: The amount of money gained in a business after the expenses are paid.

Profit and loss statement: A summary of income and expenses that shows how much profit or loss was made by a business for a certain period of time.

Project: A plan or undertaking.

Purchase order: A form used in business to record purchases of supplies.

Receipt: A written statement that something has been received or purchased.

Reclaiming: Getting something useful from waste products; making fit for use again.

Recommend: To speak good of someone; praise.

Records: Written accounts of facts for future use.

Recycling: Making a new product from old materials; reusing.

Refunder: Someone who saves labels and box tops to get cash refunds and free coupons from companies.

Related services: Services or work of the same kind or in connection with something already being done.

Reputation: Good name; well-thought-of by people.

Resale shop: A business that sells your used items for you and gives you part of the money.

Research: Careful, patient study to find out facts.

Responsibility: Something you're expected to care for or manage; duty.

Risk: To take a chance of failure or loss.

Salesmanship: Everything you do to show and sell your product.

Salesperson: One who works at selling products or services.

Sales talk: A planned presentation of information to a customer about a product or service in order to convince them to buy.

Salvage dealer: Business that buys junked or damaged items and sells the good parts to others.

Schedule: A list of times when certain things will happen; a time plan.

Scrap: Something thrown away because it is useless.

Second-hand store: A business that buys used items and sells them.

Self-employed: Earning income from your own business; working for yourself.

Service: Work done for others; help.

Short-term: For a limited, small period of time.

Slogan: A phrase or motto used by a business to describe its product and get attention.

Specialize: To have more knowledge than most people about a certain job or area of business.

Spending money: Funds available to use for things you want or need.

Stationery: Special paper and envelopes for writing, often printed with name and address.

Stencil: A pattern with holes cut where you want to paint.

Successful: Turning out well, as hoped for, or as expected.

Supplier: A business that sells items to another business for sale to the public.

System: An orderly way of doing a job.

Target customers: People who are most likely to need or want what you have to offer.

To-do list: A detailed list of everything you need to do for a certain project or period of time.

Trademark: A special picture or symbol that reminds people of a business or product.

Transaction: Business activity; carrying on business.

Update: To bring in line with the latest information.

Wholesale: Sale of goods in large amounts, usually at a discount.

Winner: A person who gets what he wants after some effort; a person who does his best to perform well.

Word-of-mouth: Happy customers telling others about your business — the best kind of advertising.

Yard sale: A home sale of used and unwanted items (usually held in the front yard).

Young entrepreneur: A person under the age of twenty-one who owns and operates a business, usually part-time.

Want to find out about other kids
who are starting businesses?

Get the *Kids Mean Business* Newsletter!

(SUBSCRIPTION INFORMATION ON NEXT PAGE)

KIDS MEAN BUSINESS

Volume 1, Issue 1   August/September 1989

KID ALERT: BIG BUCKS IN BUSINESS

Move over world. Here comes a new breed of kids ready to challenge Wall Street. Kids age 9-15 may be too young to get a job, but they are not too young to start a business.

Hundreds of letters are pouring into the KIDS MEAN BUSINESS mailbox — all from kids wanting to get their hands on the latest hot tips and plans for starting a business.

It's your newsletter, kids. We

━ Nicole Johnson (14) of Buford, GA started a calligraphy business. She does ornamental ink lettering on party invitations and poems on parchment paper. Her story was in GO Magazine.

━ Brian Whitton (14) of Corpus Christi, TX makes half pipe skate ramps for finger boards with scrap plywood and cardboard. He sells them for $3

KIDS MEAN BUSINESS

Edited by *Kid Biz* authors Bonnie and Noel Drew

A NEWSLETTER FOR YOUNG ENTREPRENEURS:

- Stories of kids who have started businesses
- Best kids' tips on saving and managing money
- Answers to surveys on kids' money questions

Receive six jam-packed issues of *Kids Mean Business* each year for only $8!

ORDER FORM

Yes, I would like to receive *Kids Mean Business* six times a year. Enclosed is $8 for one year.

NAME _____

ADDRESS _____

CITY _____

STATE _____ ZIP _____

Send orders to:

Kids Mean Business
Dept. B
1808 Capri Ln.
Seabrook, TX 77586